ECCLESIAL BEING
CONTRIBUTIONS TO THEOLOGICAL DIALOGUE

CONSTANTINE B. SCOUTERIS

Ecclesial Being

CONTRIBUTIONS TO THEOLOGICAL DIALOGUE

edited by
Christopher Veniamin

MOUNT THABOR PUBLISHING
2006

ECCLESIAL BEING: CONTRIBUTIONS TO THEOLOGICAL DIALOGUE

First published 2005
Reprinted (with minor corrections) 2006

Copyright © 2005 by Constantine B. Scouteris

Published by
Mount Thabor Publishing
PO Box 109
South Canaan, PA 18459 USA

www.thaborian.com

Printed in the United States of America

ISBN 0-9774983-1-X

Library of Congress Control Number: 2005938090

For
Basil, Chrysoula, Calliope and Constantine

CONTENTS

FOREWORD

IN HIS *Ecclesial Being*, Constantine Scouteris, Professor of Theology in the University of Athens, focuses most ably on the mystery of the human person in the context of the conciliarity of the Church. His vision of unity, based on the Pauline theme of the New Israel, embraces all Orthodox Christian peoples – wonderfully diverse in language and culture – as one nation in Christ, to which the entire world is invited to join.

This collection of studies will make Dr. Scouteris' work more readily accessible to the student interested in Orthodox ecclesiology, and bring his inspiring vision of the Church to a wider public.

C. V.

SAINT TIKHON'S ORTHODOX THEOLOGICAL SEMINARY
ENTRY OF THE MOTHER OF GOD INTO THE HOLY OF HOLIES
21 NOVEMBER, 2005

THE PEOPLE OF GOD
THE UNITY AND THE GLORY THEREOF
A DISCUSSION OF JOHN 17:17–24 IN THE LIGHT OF PATRISTIC THOUGHT*

A T THE VERY BEGINNING OF THIS ADDRESS, I would like to say what a high honour and distinct privilege it is for me to be asked to deliver the annual lecture in commemoration of the faith and testimony of Father Georges Florovsky.

The protopresbyter Georges Florovsky was a man of great theological contribution, of genuine spiritual vision, and of humble pastoral *diakonia*. In the memory of those who had the privilege of knowing him, he will remain as "an example of the believers, in word, in conversation, in charity, in spirit, in faith, in purity" (1 Tim. 4:12). In the hearts of those who have known him through his writings, he will be remembered as a theologian dedicated to bear witness to what we call "the Orthodox ethos", or "the Orthodox way". Both as a scholar and as a pastor, the late Father Georges Florovsky was a living testimony to patristic theology. His entire theological approach was according to the mind of the Fathers. His constant effort was to prove that the eternal strength of Orthodox theology lies in the patristic inheritance.

With the same intention, the Orthodox Theological Society of America, honouring his memory, projects the spirit and the passion, the life and the word of our Fathers. And, indeed, to transmit the spirit and the message of the patristic inheritance is, I believe, the best service one can offer to modern man caught up as he is in his own self-sufficiency and futility.

Status of the Question

THE stress on the patristic way, this supreme concern of Father Georges Florovsky, leads me to concentrate my attention on a theme which was often discussed by the Greek Fathers, and yet is not infrequently overlooked in our contemporary ecclesiastical life, despite the fact that it is often included in the agenda for our theological consultations. Living as we do in a society where emphasis is placed on programs and structures, we often understand the Church as an organism in the narrow sense. We pay less attention to the fact that she is a new totality, a new generation, a peculiar gathering of people, in which immense potentialities are offered to all. The world in which we live inflicts upon us a secular understanding of the Church. Thus, the fact that the Church, although in the world, is not of the world, frequently escapes our attention. In fact we do not always realize that the Church is the transcendence of the world.

When we consider the New Testament data more carefully and thoroughly we find ourselves in the presence of a new, glowing life. There is nothing in the world which offers any real parallel to this remarkable and unique life. The New Testament presents us with the possibility of realizing that ecclesiastical communion is the abolition, in the most radical way, of any worldly human communion, and is the creation of a new relationship. For me, this is summed up in the words of Christ himself: "I am come to send fire on the earth ... Suppose ye that I am come to give peace on earth? I tell you, nay, but rather division. For from henceforth there shall be five in one house divided, three against two, and two against three. The father shall be divided against the son, and the son against the father, the mother against the daughter, and the daughter against the mother, the mother-in-law against her daughter-in-law, and the daughter-in-law against her mother-in-law" (Luke 12:49–53).[1]

Before coming to grips with the issue I am going to discuss, I feel that it is necessary to say just a few words about the theme itself, and the way in which I intend to discuss it. My concern in this presentation is to argue the subject: "The people of God: its unity and its glory." It is well-known that in recent Orthodox theology, issues related to the people in general, or to the laity in particular, recur constantly. We speak very frequently about the people of God, about its importance and its authority.[2] The question is, what do we mean when we speak of the people, and where do its unity and uniqueness lie? My aim here is to touch on this issue and to present a theological outline, or if you like, a very brief theology of the people of God.

More precisely, I wish to read a concrete scriptural passage, relevant to the theme proposed, and to examine it in the light of the patristic interpretation. My intention is to draw your attention to certain aspects of the patristic understanding. However, it must be said from the beginning that I am making no claim to presenting you with a detailed analysis of every point of the biblical passage which I shall use. I shall rather be taking it as a starting point or a framework of my investigation, trying to focus my thought on its main points.

The passage of which I am speaking is drawn from the high priestly prayer of Christ. When we read this prayer in John's Gospel we find ourselves face to face with notions that are applied to God and to the people of God simultaneously. Christ is praying for his disciples, but as he adds, not "for these alone, but for them also which shall believe on me through their word." His concern is for their unity and their sanctification in the truth. "Sanctify them through thy truth; thy word is truth . . . that they all may be one; as thou, Father, art in me, and I in thee, that they also may be one in us, that the world may believe that thou hast sent me. And the glory which thou gavest me I have given them, that they may be one even as we are one and that the world may know that thou hast sent me, and hast loved them, as thou hast loved me. Father, I will that they also, whom thou hast given me, be with me where I am, that they may behold my glory, which thou hast given me" (John 17:17–24).

The Divine Oneness and the Unity of the People

EVIDENTLY, this prayer is not concerned with the future unity of the churches, but with the maintenance of that unity in glory which was given to the Apostles and to the faithful in and through Christ.[3] In fact, the prayer has two major themes: the unity of the disciples and of all those who will believe in Christ through the apostolic preaching, and their participation in the divine glory. These two points are obviously interrelated, and I believe that they constitute a solid ground for a theology of the people.

The main characteristic point of this prayer of Christ is his request for unity. The word "one" is repeated a striking number of times within a few lines. It occurs six times in four verses, and it stresses the paradoxical connection between the divine unity and the unity of those human persons who had believed in Christ. In fact, Christ stresses the reality of communion with God as the *sine qua non* for the being of man and for the oneness of all believers. Communion with the "One" is the only bond which unites the people in one particular unity.[4]

In other words, the oneness of the people of God is not understood as an autonomous and enclosed reality but as a continuous and dynamic share of the divine fullness and oneness. Or, to put it another way, the divine oneness transforms human multiplicity into a harmonious agreement. The divine oneness covers every aspect of ecclesiastical life, and although "we have many members in one body", being many we are one in Christ" (Rom. 12:4–8). I cannot find any other more characteristic and clear illustration of this than the words of Saint Ignatius when writing to the Philadelphians:

I exhort you to have but one faith, and one preaching, and one Eucharist. For there is one flesh of the Lord Jesus Christ, and his blood which was shed for us is one. One loaf also is broken for all, and one cup is distributed among them all. There is but one altar for the whole Church, and one bishop, with the presbytery and deacons. Since also there is but one unbegotten being, God, even the Father, and one only-begotten Son, God, the Word and man, and one Comforter, the Spirit of truth, and also one preaching, and one faith, and one baptism, and one Church which the holy Apostles established from one end of the earth to the other by the blood of Christ, and by their own sweat and toil, it behooves you also, therefore, as "a peculiar people, and a holy nation", to perform all things with harmony in Christ.[5]

The Old and the New Israel

IN its simplicity Saint Ignatius' argument makes it clear that the oneness of the people is made possible only through the divine oneness. The gathering of the people of God into one synagogue is thus a *koinonia* in the image of the divine communion. The people of the New Israel form a new, unbroken totality because God, freely and willingly, transcending his transcendence, created a new personal relationship with man. In the Old Israel the relationship between God and the people was a kind of subject–object relationship. God was acting behind the veil of human history. He was speaking from outside; his word was an external claim: "Hear this, all ye people, give ear all ye inhabitants of the world, both low and high, rich and poor together" (Psalm 42:1–2). Thus, the unity of the Old Israel was a result of submission to the one voice of God which came as an external law, commandment or prophetic assurance. In the New Israel the oneness of the people is the result of a *symbiosis* and *enoikesis,* of the dwelling of God among men (John 1:14). The fundamental difference between the Old and New Israel lies in the radical change from a subject–object relationship to one of participation or communion. This means that in the New Israel God no longer acts in human history as an external factor, but himself enters on the scene of human history, and becomes the central person in it. This is the meaning of "ἐσκήνωσεν ἐν ἡμῖν". Thus, by his unique *kenotic* action the divine Logos became himself history *enhypostasized.* By his self-emptying and abasement, he is involved in human history in a personal and direct way. John Zizioulas speaks of the "existential involvement" of God in human history. This "existential involvement"[6] of God in human destiny constitutes the surpassing of the law by the truth. It is in this sense that Paul spoke of the ransom (ἐξαγορά) of those who were under the law (Gal. 4:5). Hence the New Israel is in an absolutely new situation, one created by God's *kenotic* going out of himself and by his redemptive indwelling (ἐνοίκησις) in man. Clearly, this means that the unity of the new people of God resulted from the personal communion which was created by the incarnate Logos. The divine Logos became the unifying bond, the gathering of the people "from the four winds" or "from the ends of the earth".

Divine and Human Ecstasy

IN their attempt to stress the connection between the divine oneness and the oneness of the new people, the Areopagite and Saint Maximus the Confessor speak of God's ecstatic action. This divine ecstasy is understood as a movement of God, and as dwelling in the heart of human reality. Thus the Incarnation implies an exodus of God out of himself, while he yet stays within himself, in order to eliminate the existing gulf between God and man. This ecstasy or movement of God is understood in terms of divine love. "For God so loved the world, that he gave his only begotten Son" (John 3:16).

God's ecstatic love can be compared with nothing, since it is a love beyond human experience. It is a unifying and conjoining love, diametrically opposed to human love which is "a partial, physical and divided quality". While God's love is "beginningless" and "endless" revolving "in a perpetual circle for the Good, from the Good, in the Good, and to the Good", human love is a "vain image" or a "lapse" of the real love.[7] Both the author of the Areopagite texts and Maximus the Confessor prefer to use the term ἔρως in order to speak about the divine love. The term "yearning" is considered to be "more divine" and better illustrates the fact that God, although unmovable in himself, is moved in order to make man free from his divisions and his loneliness. Thus God in his yearning is transported outside of himself, and being united with human nature hypostatically, but without confusion, he transfers divine unity to the human plane. The ecstatic "emigration", so to speak, of the incarnate Logos forms the ontological basis of what we call "one body". Thus, in and through Christ man has the possibility of connecting himself with the perfect divine oneness in a personal and unique communion of love. This is what is meant, I believe, by Christ's words, "I in them, and thou in me, that they may be perfect in one." God's outgoing constitutes the presupposition and the beginning of man's going out of himself in order to meet the divine Thou and to reach a personal communion with him.

Thus, in and through Christ, the incarnate Word, we have a reciprocal *ecstasis*. God is moved by a yearning, going out of himself in order to move man towards himself. At one and the same time, he both *acts* this unique and ecstatic yearning and is the object of that yearning. He is both ἔρως and ἐραστόν. As ἔρως he goes out of himself, and as ἐραστόν he is the motive power leading towards himself all those who are able to receive his love.[8] It is within this theological context that Ignatius' words, "He for whom I yearn is crucified" (ὁ ἐμὸς ἔρως ἐσταύρωται)[9] can be understood. And it is from this perspective that we must read Paul's words, "I live, and yet not I, but Christ liveth in me" (Gal. 2:20).[10]

God's ecstatic movement towards man, and man's free response in a motion of love towards God, which is also ecstatic, form precisely the community of the new Israel. The communion of the new people in Christ is thus a meeting which is effected in a double motion, of both God and man. The *kenotic* movement of the Logos is the embracing and the unification of human nature, which is, due to sin, partial and divided. As such, it constitutes the *locus* in which every human *ego* can create its own personal and unique relationship with God. But it should be underlined once more at this point that this new communion presupposes not only the "emigration" of God, but also the "emigration" of man. Man must respond to God's offer by freely offering his own existence to him who became a "curse" (Gal. 3:13) in order to re-establish the lost communion of man with his creator. It is important, I think, to note in connection with this that, in a certain sense, man carries his fellow believers along with him through his free dedication to God. The free offering of the one results in, and provokes, the offering of the other. It is a challenge which urges others to do likewise. In other words, the offering of the one contributes to the increase and growth of the entire ecclesiastical body, and to the maturing of it. In this sense the offering of the one becomes an ecclesiological act with catholic significance. And it is precisely this offering of the one, which leads to the offering of the others, that we have in mind when we sing in the Divine Liturgy: "Let us commend ourselves and one another and our whole life to Christ our God."

The Person of the Father as the Cause of the Divine Unity

IN discussing the question of the unity of the people of God, there are some further observations to be made which may throw more light on the issue. The first point which deserves to be given more careful consideration is the connection between the divine unity and the unity of the people of God. The question is stressed clearly, as has already been pointed out, by Christ: "that they may be one, even as we are one." The divine oneness is the model for the oneness of the people. In fact, the people can be one only because the triune God is the fullness of unity.[11]

Allow me to undertake a doctrinal analysis. In the tradition of the Greek Fathers it is commonly asserted that the source, the beginning and the recapitulation of the intertrinitarian unity is the person of the Father. The oneness of God is thus understood as having a "personal" dimension, so to speak. The one God is not the inaccessible divine nature, but is the Father, the cause of the existence of the other two divine Persons. The Father, the principle of the hypostases, gives himself over to the other two divine Persons, generating the Son, and causing the Holy Spirit to proceed, thus establishing a unique unity based on his monarchy. We have to understand this "giving over" of the Father as the communication of his divine essence to the Son and to the Holy Spirit. This *ecstasis* of the Father is an action of freedom and of love. It is a personal *kenosis*, so to speak, an ἀκένωτος κένωσις of the Father for the benefit of the other two divine Persons. The Son and the Holy Spirit respond freely to this "gushing forth" of the Father's love. They neither usurp the Father's love for their own benefit, nor seize it (Phil. 2:6), but offer their existence and life to the Father in love, as he does to them. This exchange (ἀντίδοσις) in love and freedom is expressed as absolute obedience to the Father's will.[12]

I think it is clear from what has been pointed out so far that the ontological cause of the Godhead and of the divine oneness is not the divine essence, but the hypostasis of the Father. God's unity and the intertrinitarian life are not the consequence of the one nature but of the existence of the Father through whom the Son and the Holy Spirit receive their existence. "All that the Son and the Spirit have", says Saint John Damascene, "is from the Father, even their very being, and unless the Father is, neither the Son nor the Spirit is. And unless the Father possesses a certain attribute, neither the Son nor the Spirit possesses it: and through the Father, that is, because of the Father's existence, the Son and the Spirit exist, and through the Father, that is, because of the Father having the qualities, the Son and the Spirit have all their qualities."[13]

The Person of the Son as the Cause of Ecclesiastical Unity

THUS in the trinitarian life it is the person of the Father who is the sole cause of the existence of the other two divine Persons, and is consequently the unique principle of the divine communion. The person of the Father is the ontological basis of the divine communion. Likewise, in the Church it is the person of the incarnate Logos who makes every human being a unique person, thus establishing a communion of persons in the image of the three divine Persons. The incarnate Logos transferred the divine unity to the human level as a personal communion. The incarnate Logos becomes the ontological foundation of the new people. This means that there can be unity of the people because there is Christ. It is the person of the incarnate Logos who reveals the authentic human person and makes every human being a unique person in communion with others.

What does this mean? What do we mean when we say that the incarnate Logos reveals the authentic human person and creates a communion of persons? In the first instance, we simply mean that the Logos of God re-established in his person the divine image which had been obscured by sin, thus opening the way for man's liberation from his estrangement, from his isolation and individuality. It also means, however, that the foundation of the unity of the new people of God cannot be found outside personal communion. The unity of the people of God is not the consequence of a particular external teaching. The unifying force of the people of God is not theoretical agreement. Similarly, its oneness is not based on a new common law, with new commandments and regulations.

Let us state the argument again: the uniqueness of the New Testament people lies in the fact that this people (λαός) exists as a communion of persons. Its unity must be understood not in terms of human agreement, nor even of metaphysical beliefs, but as a recapitulation in the unique person of the incarnate Logos. In the final analysis this means that, if there is unity, it is because the re-creation of the human person is realized in Christ. Saint Paul puts this well in his epistle to the Ephesians, "In Christ Jesus ye who sometimes were far off are made nigh by the blood of Christ. For he is our peace, who hath made both one, and hath broken down the middle wall of partition between us, having abolished in his flesh the enmity . . . for to make in himself of twain one new man, so making peace, and that he might reconcile both unto God in one body by the cross, having slain the enmity thereby . . . Now therefore ye are no more strangers and foreigners, but fellow citizens with the saints, and of the household of God" (Eph. 2:13–19).

This passage from Paul refers primarily to the Gentiles who are "fellow heirs, and of the same body, and partakers" of the promise of God in Christ by the Gospel (Eph. 3:6). It is also signifi-cant, however, for a generally better understanding of the unity of persons in the one body of the Church. The point is that in the person of Christ all distinctions and divisions are abolished. And we know that the corruption of human nature is due to the fact that it is a rupture and a breaking off of the original unity estab-lished by God. Allow me briefly to elaborate.

The Unifying Energy of the Creator

WE are aware that when we speak of the creation we mean that God, freely and in love, exercises his personal capacity for producing entirely new beings. Creation *ex nihilo* implies that God created realities which are outside of himself, and despite the fact that there is an "infinite" distance, or rather an ontological gulf (χάσμα), between the nature of God and that of created beings, God's intention was not one of producing beings which would have no participation in his glory.

Since God [explains the Damascene], who is good and more than good, did not find satisfaction in self-contemplation, but in his exceeding goodness wished certain things to come into existence which would enjoy his benefits and share in his goodness, he brought all things into being and created them, both what is invisible and what is visible, yea, even man, who is a compound of the visible and invisible.[14]

Thus the ontological gulf between the uncreated Lord and his creatures is nullified by God's love and his immutable maintenance of all created beings. This means that despite the fact that God creates beings outside himself there is still a strong connection between himself and the created things. God abolishes the infinite distance between uncreated and created through his unifying and perfecting energy which permeates all. Again I must quote from Saint John of Damascus who speaks of the "divine radiance and activity", which although in itself "one and simple and indivisible . . . is multiplied without division among the divided, and gathers and converts the divided into its own simplicity. For all things long after it and have their existence in it. And it gives being to all things according to their several natures, and it is itself the being of existing things, the life of living things, the reason of rational beings, the thought of thinking beings. But it is itself above mind and reason and life and essence."[15]

The primordial vocation of created beings was unity with the creator. And although the created, according to its nature, is outside God, its call and ultimate destiny was to be in union with him and to share in his goodness. We must emphasize here that the connection between created and uncreated must be understood not only in terms of dependence, but also in terms of God's penetration of the universe, and of his holding and containing of it. The divine power creates, holds together and unites all beings. Saint Gregory of Nyssa is very explicit on this matter. "The divine power", he says, "skilful and wise, is manifested in beings and, pervading everything, adapts the parts to the whole, and completes the whole by the parts, and through one power holds together the universe."[16] God the creator holds all created beings together in existence and in unity and communion with himself. God, "the source of beauty and of every good", adds the Areopagite, "is the cause of all (ποιητικὸν αἴτιον), and the mover of all, and that which holds all together in the love of its beauty . . . and among beings there is nothing which does not participate in the Good and the beautiful."[17] One of the characteristic properties of the uncreated power is "to pervade and to extend to every part of the nature of beings".[18]

Although the theme of God's containing and penetrating his created beings has a philosophical background, namely Stoic and Neoplatonic,[19] the patristic understanding of it goes beyond the philosophical approach. The unity is understood by the Fathers in purely biblical and theological terms. They did not speak of it in terms of speculation, but always and constantly within a soteriological context. In fact, it is the divine "emigration" and radiance of God, the trinitarian love, which calls created beings to share the divine unity and glory.

The Destructive Character of Sin

THIS original oneness and conjunction (συνάφεια) of the universe with God, the symphony (σύμπνοια), so to speak, of all beings with one another was dissolved by sin. In order to understand the unity of the people of God better it is necessary to say a few words about the destructive character of sin. Sin introduced discord and confusion into the created universe. Even the material world suffers its effects. Sin is understood in patristic anthropology as a catastrophe caused by the free will of intelligent beings. It is a turning away which causes the entire *cosmos* to break loose from its creator. The primordial vocation was for unity, but sin introduces division.

As a matter of fact, sin is a continuous decomposition, disorganization and dissolution of the unity created by God. It is a separation and disruption in the harmony of beings. The author of the Areopagite treatises speaks of sin as "an inharmonious mingling of discordant elements."[20] Thus, in the condition of sin, man is separated from God as well as from his fellow man. This means that in the final analysis, selfhood and hate are introduced instead of *eros* for the "other" person. It is in this sense that Jean-Paul Sartre spoke of the other as "hell" and "sin." "My original fall is the existence of the other."[21] The sinful condition implies that man understands himself not as a person in connection with God and other human persons, but as an individual. Under the heavy yoke of time and space the individual man follows his own way which leads nowhere. The ideal of "my existence for the other, and the other's existence for me," is understood as an illusion, or rather as the condition for the exercise of a lie.[22] From this perspective man is the being "who is what he is not, and who is not what he is."[23] In the condition of sin the first man, instead of "being with" the other, found himself in a stage of absolute isolation "at the east of the garden of Eden" (Gen. 3:24). The words of God addressed to him, "in the sweat of thy face thou shalt eat bread" (Gen. 3:19), describe the human tragedy of opposition to God and separation from him. Thus, by the free acceptance of sin, the innate connection between man and God was destroyed. And so man, instead of loving God and being his servant, in a world of which he was designated to be prophet, priest and king,[24] became an alien and a stranger. In fact, sin consists in the limitation of man to his individuality. It is a reduction of the human person within the limits of his own existence. Thus, through sin man became a stranger to his communion with God, a stranger to his fellowship with the human "other," and even a stranger to himself. Sin, as a decomposition and separation, effects both the disorganization and the disruption of the human person itself.

The man of sin, in other words, is a divided personality. The original and innate unity of the human person is disrupted and dissolved by sin. I cannot find any clearer exposition of this division of the human person than that expounded by Paul in Romans 7:19–24.

For the good that I would I do not: but the evil which I would not, that I do. Now if I do that I would not, it is no more I that do it, but sin that dwelleth in me. I find then a law, that, when I would do good, evil is present with me. For I delight in the law of God after the inward man: But I see another law in my members, warring against the law of my mind, and bringing me into captivity to the law of sin which is in my members. O wretched man that I am! who shall deliver me from the body of this death?

The Restoration of the Human Person

THE decomposition of the human person affects the very structure of his being. It is, as Gregory of Nyssa would say, a real *"analysis"* of man.[25] The original unity of soul and body became uncertain and unstable through sin. In short, sin abolishes man as a person. It is a decomposition of his very being; it makes him live this divided and disorganized life only for himself, and thus it deprives him of the possibility of living in fellowship with others and with God. It is only through the self-emptying of the person of the Logos of God that a new creation and restructuring of the human person can be realized. Saint Gregory of Nyssa uses the term ἀναστοιχείωσις to stress the radical change effected in the very structure of man's existence. The restoration or, even better, the recombination of the human person results from the person of the incarnate Logos, and consequently its authentic state of κοινωνία is re-established. Just as evil "was poured into a multitude of persons by one man through succeeding generations", similarly "the good begotten in human nature was bestowed upon every person as one entity."[26] Saint Maximus the Confessor likes to explain that "that which was absolutely immovable according to nature, moved, and God became man in order to save the lost man." Salvation is understood in terms of unification of the divided human nature. Thus the divine Logos, through his self-emptying, re-establishes the ancient harmony of nature. By his penetration of man's nature Christ brings together the divided parts of our nature, so as to form one perfect unity again.[27] Indeed, Christ is the gathering of all together in one (Eph. 1:10).

At this point I would like to underline the fact that the unification of man's divided nature is an act of God which is "personal". Let me elaborate very briefly on this. Earlier in this paper I tried to explain that, according to the patristic understanding, the basis of the divine unity is the person of the Father, not the inaccessible divine essence. I also tried to explain that, in an analogous way, the unity of the people of God is founded on the person of the incarnate Logos. This means that unity, both as intertrinitarian communion as well as fellowship of the people in Christ, is not an "ontological necessity", due to either the nature of God as regards divine unity, or to human nature as regards unity in the Church. The people are one not because they all belong to and share in the same nature, but because, through the personal abasement of the second divine person, they themselves become persons, thus sharing in the personal life of Christ. It is the person of Christ, not an impersonal divinity, who re-establishes human persons.

The notion of "person" is an essential Christian concept, based on the reality of God being personal, and on the fact that man has been created in the divine image in order not to be confined in his own self, but to share the divine life, in fellowship with others.

And, although the term *prosopon* is well known in classical Greek antiquity, it is only in Christian thought, namely in the Greek patristic tradition, that it finds its theological content. Neither in the Aristotelian system, nor in Platonic philosophy, nor in the Stoics, nor even in the revival of the Platonic tradition in Middle and Neoplatonism, does the notion of "person" acquire a satisfactory and solid meaning.

The inability of Greek philosophy to give a positive answer to the question of personality lies in the fact that the person is understood as an exclusively human and worldly reality. According to the Greeks the person is limited within the boundaries of time and space. It is always under the heavy yoke of time and space that all people of all generations move along. And even the gods themselves are presented as being prisoners of this double yoke. Thus the human personality pulling time and space becomes a tragic phenomenon. Ancient Greek tragedy vividly expresses the drama of the human being who, pushed by some invisible force, follows a path of sufferings, afflictions and pain. The use of masks in the Greek tragedies expresses nothing other than man's strong desire to surpass and to free himself from his destiny. The ancient world presents us with a depersonalized human person without hope, a moribund human person who, under the yoke of time and space, constantly suffers the pangs of death, and yet never dies. This is a human person under the dominion of sin and death. We can speak of sin as the power which deprives man of his authentic person. Saint Gregory of Nyssa says that through sin man has changed the image of God, that is his real person, with a mask (προσωπεῖον).[28] It is the Christian Gospel which reveals the true dimension of the human person. In and through the Gospel, human tragedy is transfigured into a new reality. This transfiguration is understood in terms of re-creation of the hidden and obscured human person. Saint Gregory of Nyssa speaks again about the repainted and restored image of God.[29] Thus the importance and the uniqueness of the Gospel lies in the fact that the human impasse as presented in the Greek tragedies has been overcome. Through all life's afflictions and pains man can now

hear the consoling voice of God manifested in the flesh: "Come
unto me all ye that labour and are heavy laden, and I will give you
rest. Take my yoke upon you, and learn of me, for I am meek and
lowly in heart: and ye shall find rest unto your souls. For my yoke
is easy, and my burden is light" (Matt. 11:28–30).

The Unity of the People – A Unity of Persons

THE point which I am trying to make is that the unity of the
people of God is a unity of persons. This means precisely that the
unity of the ecclesiastical body is not the result of the coexistence
of certain individuals who accept the same theoretical or moral
principles, but is indeed a communion of those who share freely,
and in the measure which has been given to them, in the life of
the divine persons. As a matter of fact the notion of personality is
understood by the Greek Fathers as being a primarily theological
notion. In the final analysis this means that outside God the idea
of the person is an illusion. In other words, the authentic person
is an uncreated reality. Because the person is uncreated reality, it
is absolutely free from every necessity, even from the "necessity"
(if we can speak in this way) of its own nature. It is within this
theological context that we can understand the persistent efforts
of the Greek Fathers to maintain that the principle of divine unity
is the person of the Father, and not the common divine nature.
The person of the Father is the bond of trinitarian unity, because
he freely confers his own nature on the Son and on the Holy
Spirit, thus establishing a peculiar and unique divine union and
communion. And it is again within this theological context that
the fact can be better understood that, in his self-emptying, the
eternal Logos of God dwelt among us freely in order to realize in
his theandric person the restoration (ἀποκατάστασις) of the human
person. This means that, in other words, the unity and community
of persons in the Church is possible because the second divine
person became one of us, by taking one individual and concrete
human nature. Thus, the Logos of God, con-substantial with the
Father through divinity, becoming consubstantial with us through
humanity, recreated the human person and transferred the divine

unity to the human level. Therefore the unity of the people is, as we have already pointed out, the reflection and the image of divine communion; or, to put it in more conciliar terminology, the unity of the people of God is precisely theandric. I think that we can see the theandric character of the people of God in the words of Christ himself, as they were preserved by John: "I in them, and thou in me, that they may be made perfect in one" (John 17:23).

In the light of what has been pointed out so far it is, I think, clear that the true stature of the human person is exhibited in and through Christ. I believe it is also clear that the union of the people of God, this peculiar communion of persons, is possible only "ἐν Χριστῷ". It is only in Christ that we are offered the possibility of seeing what God is, both in his personal character as well as in his relationship to us. The "ἐν Χριστῷ" is therefore the necessary presupposition for the unity of human persons in the one body of the Church. The "ἐν Χριστῷ" means that the communion of the people of God is neither simply a humanitarian fellowship, nor even a company of believers, but is indeed the one body of the incarnate God; the body which is maintained in its integrity by the continuing presence of Christ and the Holy Spirit throughout the course of human history.

Unity in the Holy Spirit – Faith and the Sacraments

THE fact that Christ is present in the midst of his flock in every historical "now", evidently implies that the unity of the people is based, not on an abstract agreement, but on a direct and personal relationship. This relationship is established through the Holy Spirit, by faith and in the sacraments. "By one Spirit are we all baptized into one body" (1 Cor. 12:13). "We being many are one bread, and one body: for we are all partakers of that one bread" (1 Cor. 10:17). "One body, and one Spirit . . . one Lord, one faith, one baptism" (Eph. 4:4–5). Thus, by faith and in the sacraments, Christ assumes in the Holy Spirit our personal existence and permits us to be in communion with him, that is, to participate existentially in his own life. In this sense the unity in the body of the Church is not a one-sided unity, nor is it unconditionally given, but it implies man's personal affirmation of the personal call of God. The personal involvement of Christ in human destiny calls for our personal existence to be incorporated into his Body. The reconstruction of human existence and the unity of the "new man" are realized at the personal level by the act of acceptance of the life of Christ and especially of the central fact of this unique life, that is the death and the resurrection. Therefore, in order to transmit into his own *ego* the unification realized in the hypostasis of the incarnate Logos, man must accept existentially the ἄπαξ, the once and for all event, of Christ's death and resurrection. "So many of us as were baptized into Jesus Christ were baptized into his death. Therefore we are buried with him by baptism into death: that like as Christ was raised up from the dead by the glory of the Father, even so we also should walk in newness of life" (Rom. 6:3–4). Through baptism, therefore, life and resurrection, which were achieved by Christ's voluntary death, are realized in the very existence of man. By going through the mystery of Christ's death and resurrection, every believer is clothed in him. Obviously the death of the believer in baptism is a symbol and an imitation of real death. And although the death is not real but only an image, its consequences are those of a real transcendence of death. Here lies the mystery of the restoration of the human person and of its glory in the Church. Through imitation and a symbolic act man receives the gifts of the resurrection.

It is interesting to recall in this connection the point made by Saint Symeon the New Theologian. Although Saint Symeon follows the traditional teaching of the Fathers on sacramental baptism and recognizes it as an act of therapy, regeneration and renewal of the human person, he also speaks of a second baptism which he calls "baptism in the Holy Spirit". This second baptism is a stage in the Christian life which insures and maintains the effect of the sacramental baptism. The second baptism affirms the uniqueness and significance of the first. It is, so to speak, a testimony to, or a continuous presence of the gifts provided by sacramental baptism. As a matter of fact this second baptism is nothing other than that repentance which offers to the individual Christian a deeper understanding of his Christian consciousness, and a greater awareness of Christ as Lord and Saviour.[30] This baptism in the Holy Spirit presupposes the personal *kenosis* of the believer in repentance, and indeed it is the medium for the accomplishment in the Holy Spirit of his final goal, that is, of deification. "Display a worthy penitence", argues Saint Symeon, "by means of all sorts of deeds and words, that you may draw unto yourselves the grace of the all-holy Spirit. For this Spirit, when he descends on you, becomes like a pool of light to you, which encompasses you completely in an unutterable manner. As it regenerates you, it changes you from corruptible to incorruptible, from mortal to immortal, from sons of man into sons of God and gods by adoption and grace."[31]

It is of special interest for our study here to look at the way in which Saint Symeon connects baptism in the Spirit with the unity of the people of God. His exposition is basically a synthesis of New Testament material, and the unity of which we are speaking is presented as a trinitarian dwelling. In order to clarify his position, Saint Symeon uses the image of the house, of the door of the house, and of the key to the door. The key to the door, he explains, is the Holy Spirit "because through him and in him we are first enlightened in mind. We are purified and illuminated with the light of knowledge. We are baptized from on high and born anew [*cf.* John 3:3–5] and made into children of God."[32] The door of the house is the Son himself, "'for', says he, 'I am the door: by me if any man enter in, he shall be saved, and shall go in and out, and find pasture'" (John 10:9).[33] Finally, the house itself is the Father. Christ spoke of this when he said, "in my Father's house are many mansions" (John 14:2).[34]

Saint Symeon is here engaged in pointing out explicitly that participation in the divine glory is effected in and through the Holy Spirit. He uses this image in order to guide man to a deeper understanding of the significance of baptism in the Spirit. According to him the crucial thing to do is to understand that only in and through the Holy Spirit do we know God, do we become his children and partakers of his ineffable light. It is precisely this dwelling of the Holy Spirit in the human person which constitutes his divine adoption and inner transfiguration. It is within this context that we can understand Paul's words, "The Spirit himself intercedes for us with groanings which cannot be uttered" (Rom. 8:26), and again, "God hath sent forth the Spirit of his Son into your hearts, crying, Abba, Father" (Gal. 4:6).

Bearing in mind what has been pointed out so far we reach the conclusion that the Holy Spirit was sent to the world, in the name of the Son, to bear witness (John 15:23), and to guide human persons to him, and through him to the Father of Lights. Saint Symeon argues:

> In theological terms we use the term *house* of the Son, even as we use it of the Father, for he says, "Thou, O Father, art in me, and I in them, and they in me, and I, O Father, in thee, that we may be one" (*cf.* John 17:21,23), together with the Holy Spirit. He also says, "I will live in them and move among them" (2 Cor. 6:16). . . . I and the Father will come and make our home with him (John 14:23) through the Holy Spirit.[35]

Nevertheless, it is true that not only in Saint Symeon the New Theologian's trinitarian theology but also in the entire patristic tradition, a strong conviction exists that the Holy Spirit effects the integrity of the divided human person and the restoration of disunited humanity. The Paraclete enters the world to be the unifying principle of the new kingdom, the one force which guides all believers to the one faith and the one Lord. In fact, the Holy Spirit himself is the enhypostasized kingdom,[36] and he makes of the people a "royal priesthood" and "a holy nation" (1 Pet. 2:9). To quote Maximus:

> Thus, men, women and children profoundly divided as to race, nation, language, manner of life, work, knowledge, honour, fortune ... the Church recreates all of them in the Spirit. To all equally she communicates a divine aspect. All receive from her a unique nature which cannot be broken asunder, a nature which no longer permits one henceforth to take into consideration the many and profound differences which are their lot. In that way all are raised up and united in a manner which is truly catholic. In her, none is in the least degree separated from the community, all are grounded, so to speak, in one another by the simple and indivisible power of faith.[37]

Life in the Holy Spirit presupposes faith ("He that believeth and is baptized shall be saved" [Mark 16:16]), coexists with faith

("The Spirit itself beareth witness with our spirit, that we are the children of God" [Rom. 8:16]), and maintains faith ("No man can say that Jesus is the Lord, but by the Holy Ghost" [1 Cor. 12:3]).[38] This means that the one faith of the people is an acceptance neither of certain metaphysical axioms, nor of a set of laws given to men for their moral betterment by a God who acts authoritatively behind the scene of human activity. Faith implies an existential agreement in the Holy Spirit. It is "a fruit of the Spirit", a *charisma* (Gal. 5:22), to which man responds in a deeply personal way. "Our faith, brethren", claim the Orthodox patriarchs of the East in their famous Encyclical of 1848, "is neither from man nor by man".[39] And it is for precisely this reason that the people of God, as a whole, possesses a spiritual sense which makes it a "defender of the faith".[40]

It is very important to stress in connection with this that faith "by the Holy Spirit" is not understood exclusively as a possession on the individual level; rather, it finds its significance in the context of the ecclesiastical community. In other words, personal faith is in absolute harmony with the faith of the Catholic Church. This means that the faith of each human individual in the one body of the Church becomes truly Orthodox when it is identified with the catholic conscience of the Church, and is expressed as *consensus fidelium*.

Life in the Holy Spirit, that is the life of persons who are bound together by one baptism, one faith and identity of experience, is fulfilled in the eucharistic gathering. The eucharistic assembly is the concrete manifestation of the communion with God in Christ and in the Holy Spirit. It is the realization, through the invocation of the Holy Spirit by the Church, of the one body. When we are fed, according to Nicholas Cabasilas, with the most sacred Bread and do drink the most Divine Cup, we do partake of the same flesh and the same blood our Lord has assumed, and so are united with him who was for us incarnate, and died, and rose again.[41]

The Eucharist is the transcendence of every division; it constitutes the restoration of the ancient symphony between God and man. In it each participant exists as a person in communion both with God and with other human persons. By partaking of the bread and wine one becomes simultaneously both a communicant of the whole Christ, who is "broken and not disunited", and a communicant of the entire

Church. Or to put it better, in the Eucharist every human person becomes the *totus Christus* and the entire Church. Thus the bread of the Eucharist constitutes the central point of ecclesiastical unity. Indeed, the Eucharist is the historical realization of Christ's words, "I in them, and thou in me, that they may be made perfect in one" (John 17:23). The bread being eaten by man in his fallen condition, "in the sweat of [his] face" (Gen. 3:19), shows, and in fact maintains his isolation and individuality. In contrast to this the eucharistic bread, by the power of the Holy Spirit, maintains the unity of human persons in Christ.

The Glory Which Thou Gavest Me I Have Given Them

WHEN we stress the fact that the Holy Spirit creates unity in Christ, and when we attempt to understand this unity in terms of a relationship, we come again to the crucial point of the entrance and dwelling of the Holy Spirit in the human reality. The Holy Spirit's permeation of the ecclesiastical body constitutes the glory and the kingship of the people, since the Holy Spirit himself is kingship and glory. In his prayer for unity Christ stresses his relationship with the Spirit, and the fact that his relationship with the Father can be reproduced by the Spirit, in an analogous way, in the lives of those who follow him. "The glory thou gavest me I have given them; that they may be one, even as we are one" (John 17:22). "Christ's own glory", as Saint Gregory of Nyssa points out, "is meant to be the Holy Spirit which he has given to his disciples by breathing upon them, for what is scattered cannot otherwise be united unless joined together by the Holy Spirit's unity." Thus Christ, by the Holy Spirit, bestows his own life on the lives of all who are willing and able to receive him. Christ can be reached only through the Spirit. "If any man have not the Spirit of Christ, he is not of his" (Rom. 8:9). The Spirit is glory, as Christ himself pointed out when he was addressing his Father: "Glorify thou me in thine own presence with the glory which I had with thee before the world was" (John 17:5). When Saint Gregory of Nyssa comments on this passage from John, he makes the following clarification: "The Logos is God who has the Father's glory. But because in these last days he became flesh, it was necessary for the flesh to become what the Logos ever was (that is, to become divine) by being united to him. And precisely this was effected when the flesh received that which the Logos had before the world was made. And this is none other than the Holy Spirit, that same Holy Spirit existing before the ages together with the Father and the Son."[42]

If we read Christ's statement, "the glory thou gavest me I have given them" (John 17:22) in this hermeneutical context, we can easily understand where the ultimate criterion of the oneness of the people lies. The mystery of Christian existence and fellowship is based on, and connects with, the personal and dynamic presence in the ecclesiastical body of the "heavenly King, the Lord, the giver of life". "Now the Lord is that Spirit: and where the Spirit of the Lord is, there is liberty. But we all, with open face beholding as in a glass the glory of the Lord, are changed into the same image from glory to glory, even as by the Spirit of the Lord" (2 Cor. 3:17-18).[43]

NOTES

* The Father Georges Florovsky Memorial Lecture of 1985, sponsored by the Orthodox Theological Society of America, first published in *The Greek Orthodox Theological Review* 30, no. 4 (1985), 399–420.

1. See also Matt. 10:34–35.

2. Thus, we often make statements such as: "The apostolic preaching is protected within the entire ecclesiastical body", or "The people of God in its entirety is the bearer of tradition", and so on.

3. See the comments of Saint Gregory of Nyssa in his treatment of 1 Cor. 15:28: *When all things shall be subdued unto him,* in *Patrologia Graeca* (PG) 44:1321A ff.

4. Μίαν οὖν τινα καὶ ἁπλῆν τῆς εἰρηνικῆς ἑνώσεως θεωρήσωμεν φύσιν, ἑνοῦσαν ἅπαντα ἑαυτῇ καὶ ἑαυτοῖς καὶ ἀλλήλοις, καὶ διασώζουσαν πάντα ἐν ἀσυγχύτῳ πάντων συνοχῇ καὶ ἀμηγῇ καὶ συγκεκραμένα, Pseudo-Dionysius, *On the Divine Names* (PG 3:949C). This unity is often called ἐνοείδεια in the writings of the Areopagite, i.e. a unity of a single form, of one and the same kind and character.

5. Chapter 4.

6. See J. Zizioulas, "The Authority of the Bible", *The Ecumenical Review* 21 (1969), 162 ff.

7. *On the Divine Names* (PG 3:709BC).

8. Ὡς μὲν ἔρως ὑπάρχον τὸ θεῖον καὶ ἀγάπη κινεῖται, ὡς δὲ ἐραστὸν καὶ ἀγαπητὸν κινεῖ πρὸς ἑαυτὸ πάντα τὰ ἔρωτος καὶ ἀγάπης δεκτικά, Maximus the Confessor, *Difficulties* (PG 91:1260C).

9. *To the Romans* 6. See also Pseudo-Dionysius, *On the Divine Names* (PG 3:709B).

10. *Ibid.* (PG 3:712A).

11. In the life of the superessential and life-giving Trinity, unity appears not as an additional or compound category, but as an absolutely radical reality which is beyond conjunctions and divisions. The number "One" as an arithmetical category is insufficient to describe the divine unity. Unity as a mathematical concept presupposes compoundness. But we know, explains Saint John of Damascus, that only those which are "composed of imperfect elements must necessarily be compound". We also know that "compoundness is the beginning of separation". However, there is nothing in the intertrinitarian life which is imperfect, or which compounds, or which leads to separation. The three divine hypostases are absolutely perfect, and consequently no compound can arise from them. The three divine Persons are united is such a way "not so as to commingle, but so as to cleave to each other, and they have their being in each other without any coalescence or commingling". While each divine hypostasis is perfect in himself, and has his own mode of existence, "each one of them is related as closely to the others as to himself". *On the Orthodox Faith* 1 (PG 94:824A–828C).

12. See my article, "*Paradosis*: The Orthodox Understanding of Tradition", *Sobornost Incorporating Eastern Churches Review* 4 (1983), 31 [reprinted in the present edition].

13. *On the Orthodox Faith* 1 (PG 94:824AB).

14. *Ibid.*, 2 (864C–865A).

15. *Ibid.*, 1 (860C).

16. *On the Soul and the Resurrection* (PG 46:28A). For fuller details, see D. L. Balas, *Μετουσία Θεοῦ: Man's Participation in God's Perfections according to Saint Gregory of Nyssa* (Rome, 1966), pp. 115–120.

17. *On the Divine Names* (PG 3:701C–704B).

18. Gregory of Nyssa, *Great Catechism* (ed. J. H. Srawley, pp. 118,[10]–119,[3]; PG 45:80D).

19. See J. Dupont, *Gnosis: La connaissance religieuse dans les épîtres de St. Paul* (Louvain, 1960), pp. 461–468, esp. 463–466. See also, Balas, *op. cit.*, p. 117.

20. *On the Divine Names* (PG 3:809BC).

21. *Being and Nothingness. A Phenomenological Essay on Orthodoxy*, trans. H. E. Barnes (New York, 1956), p. 352.

22. *Ibid.*, p. 88.

23. *Ibid.*, p. 100.

24. See G. Florovsky, "The Darkness of Night", *Creation and Redemption* (Belmont MA, 1976), p. 85.

25. "Εἰς γῆν διὰ τῆς ἁμαρτίας ἀναλυθέντος", in *When all things shall be subdued unto him* (PG 44:1312A).

26. *Ibid.* (1312B).

27. "... κινεῖται τὸ πάντη κατὰ φύσιν ἀκίνητον, καὶ Θεὸς ἄνθρωπος γίνεται, ἵνα σώσῃ τὸν ἀπολόμενον ἄνθρωπον, καὶ τῆς κατὰ τὸ πᾶν καθόλου φύσεως δι᾽ ἑαυτοῦ τὰ κατὰ φύσιν ἑνώσας ῥήγματα, καὶ τοὺς καθόλου τῶν ἐπὶ μέρους προσφερουμένους λόγους, οἷς ἡ τῶν διῃρημένων γίνεσθαι πέφυκεν ἕνωσις, δείξας τὴν μεγάλην βουλὴν πληρώσῃ τοῦ Θεοῦ καὶ Πατρός, εἰς ἑαυτὸν ἀνακεφαλαιώσας τὰ πάντα τὰ ἐν τῷ οὐρανῷ καὶ τὰ ἐπὶ τῆς γῆς, ἐν ᾧ καὶ ἐκτίσθησαν. Ἀμέλει τοι τῆς καθόλου τῶν πάντων πρὸς ἑαυτὸν ἑνώσεως, ἐκ τῆς ἡμῶν ἀρξάμενος διαιρέσεως γίνεται τέλειος ἄνθρωπος, ἐξ ἡμῶν δι᾽ ἡμᾶς καθ᾽ ἡμᾶς ..." *Difficulties* (PG 91:1308D–1309A).

28. *On the Creation of Man* (PG 44:193C). For further discussion on the subject of "person", see C. Giannaras, *Τὸ ὀτολογικὸν περιεχόμενον τῆς θεολογικῆς ἐννοίας τοῦ προσώπου* (Athens, 1970); and J. Zizioulas, "Ἀπὸ τὸ προσωπεῖον εἰς τὸ πρόσωπον· Ἡ συμβολὴ τῆς πατερικῆς θεολογίας εἰς τὴν ἔννοιαν τοῦ προσώπου", *Χαριστήρια εἰς τιμὴν τοῦ Μητροπολίτου Γέροντος Χαλκηδόνος Μελίτωνος* (Thessalonica, 1977).

29. See my book, *Consequences of the Fall and the Font of Regenration: From the Anthropology of Saint Gregory of Nyssa* (Athens, 1973), pp. 165–169 [in Greek].

26   *Constantine Scouteris*

30. *Discourses* 32, 77–84 (*Sources Chrétiennes* (*SC*) 113:244; ed. B. Krivocheine).

31. *Ibid.*, 78–85 (*SC* 113:244); Eng. trans. C. J. deCatanzaro, *Symeon the New Theologian: The Discourses*, in the series *Classics of Western Spirituality* (New York, 1980), p. 337.

32. *Ibid.*, 153–157 (*SC* 113:260); deCatanzaro, p. 343. And see also 97–99 (*SC* 113:256); deCatanzaro, p. 341.

33. *Ibid.*, 95–96 (*SC* 113:256); deCatanzaro, p. 341.

34. *Ibid.*, 100–101 (*SC* 113:256); deCatanzaro, pp. 341–342.

35. *Ibid.*, 160–176 (*SC* 113:260–262); deCatanzaro, p. 343 [revised: deCatanzaro's translation is incorrect].

36. Βασιλεία ζῶσα καὶ οὐσιώδης καὶ ἐνυπόστατος τὸ Πνεῦμα τὸ Ἅγιον, Gregory of Nyssa, *Against the Macenonians*, ed. F. Müller, *Gregorii Nysseni opera III: 1. Opera dogmatica minora* (Leiden, 1958), p. 102, 27–30; PG 45:1321A.

37. *Mystagogy* 1 (PG 91:665–668). Quoted by V. Lossky, *The Mystical Theology of the Eastern Church* (Plymouth, 1957), pp. 164–165.

38. "... ἡ ὁμολογία τῆς τοῦ Υἱοῦ κυριότητος, ἐν Πνεύματι Ἁγίῳ τοῖς καταλαμβάνουσι γίνεται, πάντοθεν τοῖς διὰ πίστεως προσεγγίζουσι προαπαντῶτος τοῦ Πνεύματος ... ἀλλὰ χρὴ τὴν εἰς τὸν Κύριον προϋποκεῖσθαι πίστιν, δι᾽ ἧς ἡ ζωτικὴ χάρις τοῖς πιστεύσασι παραγίνεται ... Ἀλλ᾽ ἐπειδὴ καὶ ἡ διὰ τοῦ Υἱοῦ διακονουμένη χάρις ἤρτηται τῆς ἀγεννήτου πηγῆς, διὰ τοῦτο προηγεῖσθαι τὴν εἰς τὸ ὄνομα τοῦ Πατρὸς πίστιν ὁ λόγος διδάσκει, τοῦ ζωογονοῦντος τὰ πάντα," Gregory of Nyssa, *Against the Macenonians, op. cit.*, p. 103, 8–106; PG 45:1321B–1325A.

39. J. N. Karmiris, *Τὰ δογματικὰ καὶ συμβολικὰ μνημεῖα τῆς Ὀρθοδόξου Καθολικῆς Ἐκκλησίας* [The Dogmatic and Symbolic Monuments of the Orthodox Catholic Church], Vol. 2 (Graz, 1968), p. 1002.

40. *Ibid.*, p. 1000.

41. *Cf.* Chapter 4 on the Holy Eucharist in *The Life in Christ*.

42. *When all things shall be subdued unto him* (PG 44:1320D). See also *Against the Macenonians*, pp. 108, 30–109, 15; PG 45:1329AB; *On Prayer* (PG 44:1157CD); *Song of Songs*, ed. H. Langerbeck, *Gregorii Nysseni opera VI: In Canticum canticorum* (Leiden, 1960), pp. 446, 14–447, 17; PG 44:1116D–1117B.

43. Saint John Chrysostom commenting on this passage makes the following observations: "... and not only do we behold the glory of God, but from it also receive a sort of splendour. Just as if pure silver were turned towards the sun's rays, it would itself also shoot forth rays, not from its own natural property merely but also from the solar lustre; so also does the soul, being cleansed and made brighter than silver, receive a ray from the glory of the Spirit, and send it back. Wherefore also he said, 'beholding as in a glass the glory of the Lord, we are changed into the same image from glory', that of the Spirit, 'to glory', our own, that which is generated in us; and of such a kind as one might expect from the Lord the Spirit." *Homily on 2 Corinthians* (PG 61:44B).

THE CHURCH
"FILLED WITH THE HOLY TRINITY"*

B EFORE I BEGIN MY PAPER, I would like to say what a
great honour and exceptional privilege it is for me to take
part in this Conference on the subject of the outstanding
and unique mystery of the Church.

Some Introductory Clarifications

ECCLESIOLOGY was always at the heart of Orthodox Theology,
because the Church was understood in Eastern Christendom
as the household of God (1 Tim. 3:15), the body of Christ,
"the fulness of him that filleth all in all" (Eph. 1:23), and as the
"dwelling place of God in the Spirit" (Eph. 2:22). Thus, first in
the New Testament, and then in the teaching of the Fathers, the
doctrine concerning the Church is steadfastly inseparable and
intertwined with Theology, Christology and Pneumatology. This
bond makes the Church a great mystery (Eph. 5:32), "the Church
of the living God" (1 Tim. 3:16), "without doubt, the great mystery
of godliness" (*cf.* 1 Tim. 3:16).

In a post-Byzantine Church in Cyprus there is a remarkable
fresco, just above the Holy Altar, representing the scene of the

eucharistic communion. On the left side one sees Christ offering the bread to His disciples, while on the right He is offering the wine. One can also see written on each side the words of the Lord: "Take, eat; this is my body", and so forth (as in the Divine Liturgy); "Drink ye all of it; For this is my blood of the new testament", and so on (as found in the Divine Liturgy, *cf.* Matt. 26:26–27). Just above this visual representation of the Eucharist is written: "This house was built by the Father. This house was made firm by the Son. This house has been renewed by the Holy Spirit." In the Orthodox tradition there is a strong conviction that the ecclesial communion is a gift of the One God in Trinity.

When the Alexandrian Origen, already in the third century, characterized the Church as "filled with the Holy Trinity", he wanted to show that a person who is within the Church dwells within the universe and belongs to the universe. "The sinner dwells in the desert. The person who is within the Church, which is filled with the Holy Trinity, dwells within the universe, which is the Church."[1] The identification of the Church with the universe and the awareness of the Church as the fulfilment of the life-giving Trinity is a basis for us to formulate two basic introductory remarks, which will help us determine the framework of our paper.

First of all, we must stress the fact that the Church is communion and life. We must at the very beginning make clear that any discussion concerning the ecclesial communion has to be based on the fact that the Church is a mystery attached to the mystery of Christ. The Church is intimately connected with the Person who joined humanity and divinity, as it is accurately expressed in the Chalcedonian definition, "without confusion, without change, without division and without separation".[2] Consequently, knowledge about the Church is not a concept that one can acquire with a particular form of academic education. Knowledge about the Church is another form of knowledge, which is achieved through the experience of communion with God. The more the human persons are immersed in the life of the Church community, the more their *nous* is illuminated and they can acquire the ecclesial consciousness. It is not by chance or without importance that the same fact of the Church is contained in one of the headings of faith in the Nicene-Constantinopolitan Creed. Since the authority of the Church pertains to One God in Trinity, following the confession of faith in One God, God the Father, God the Son and God the Holy Spirit, faith in "One holy, catholic and apostolic Church" ensues as a natural consequence. Thus, the knowledge of the mystery of the Church is revealed through faith alone, to those who have learnt to live within the Church, to see with the eyes of the Church, to hear with the ears of the Church, and to feel with the "feelings" (αἰσθήματα) of the Church.

Consequently, the Church is not known through the usual methods used to grasp an object of knowledge, but from within, with personal experience and an increase in the life of grace. The more a person immerses himself in the life of the Church, the more he becomes aware existentially, not just conceptually, of "the riches of the glory" of Christ. The more he is "strengthened with might in his spirit through the inner man", so that he "may be able to comprehend with all the saints what is the breadth, and length, and depth, and height" and "the love of Christ which passes knowledge", the more he is filled with "all the fullness of God" (Eph. 3:14–19).

The second essential remark is that the Church is not some closed religious corporation, a closed isolated religious community, but rather an open embrace, since God is the "Saviour of all men" (1 Tim. 4:10) and "will have all men to be saved, and to come unto the knowledge of the truth" (1 Tim. 2:4). Often, in Christian circles there seems to be a sense of caution and introversion. Perhaps this is from the suddenness of rapid social transformation, maybe even today from some inclination towards self-defence in the face of the manifold provocations brought about by secularization and globalization on a material basis. It is an unjustifiable feeling of self-complacency, and a contraction and lessening of the Church. Thus, an insurmountable wall is raised, which isolates the Church and alienates it from its universal dimension.

The persistent endeavour of the Fathers to prove that the cross of Christ is raised in every age and in every place on earth is illustrative. The cross is the visible symbol of the Church and the actual point of salvation of the whole world in Christ. It is a reminder in all directions, that the Victor over the cross and death, "resurrected with him all the race of Adam from the grave".[3] With His sacrifice on the cross Christ became "the propitiation for our sins: and not for ours only, but also for the sins of the whole world" (1 John. 2:2). Saint John Chrysostom would say that with the appearance of the cross and the resurrection of Christ "the universe was cleansed".[4]

The ever memorable professor, John Karmiris, of the University of Athens, notes that in our time, a time of division between Christians and non-Christians, Orthodox, heterodox and heretics, the Cross of Christ is raised up. "The brilliance and the saving grace of the cross is not only aimed at all Orthodox Christians, but beyond them its rays shine out to all the non-Christians, the gentiles, the idolaters, and even more so towards heterodox Christians and heretics, all of them children of the same heavenly Father, for whom Christ 'died for all' (2 Cor. 5:14–15). . . . Thus, the ark of salvation, the Church, is expanded and embraces the whole world. It is mysteriously extended on the one hand from here to the heterodox Christians and heretics, on the other from here to non-Christians and followers of different religions, of whom those who are distinguished for their faith in God, moved by love, are 'brought near' to the Church 'by the blood of Christ' (Eph. 2:13)."[5]

This attitude is illustrated by an event, related by Staretz Sophrony, involving Saint Silouan the Athonite:

"I remember a conversation he [Saint Silouan] had with a certain Archimandrite who was engaged in missionary work [amongst the heterodox]. This Archimandrite thought highly of the Staretz and many a time went to see him on his visits to the Holy Mountain. The Staretz asked what sort of sermons he preached to the people. The Archimandrite who was still young and inexperienced, gesticulated with his hands and swayed his whole body, and replied excitedly,

"'I tell them, Your faith is all wrong, perverted. There is nothing right, and if you don't repent there will be no salvation for you.'

"The Staretz [Saint Silouan] heard him out, then asked,

"'Tell me, Father Archimandrite, do they believe in the Lord Jesus Christ, that He is the true God?'

"'Yes, that they do believe.'

"'And do they revere the Mother of God?'

"'Yes, but they are not taught properly about her.'

"'And what of the Saints?'

"'Yes, they honour them, but since they have fallen away from the Church, what saints can they have?'

"'Do they celebrate the Divine Office in their churches? Do they read the Gospels?'

"'Yes, they do have churches and services but if you were to compare their services with ours – how cold and lifeless they are!'

"'Father Archimandrite, people feel in their souls when they are doing the proper thing, believing in Jesus Christ, revering the Mother of God and the Saints, whom they call upon in prayer, so if you condemn their faith they will not listen to you . . . But if you were to confirm that they were doing well to believe in God and honour the Mother of God and the Saints; that they are right to go to church, and say their prayers at home, read the Divine word, and so on; and then gently point out their mistakes and show them what they ought to amend, then they would listen to you, and the Lord would rejoice over them. And this way, by God's mercy we shall all find salvation . . . God is love, and therefore the preaching of His word must always proceed from love. Then both preacher and listener will profit. But if you do nothing but condemn, the soul of the people will not heed you, and no good will come of it.'"[6]

The "ecclesiastification" of the whole human race is based on the fact that with his Incarnation, the Son of God, taking on a particular individual human nature accordingly took on the whole of our human make-up and became of the same essence according to his humanity with all human beings. On the basis of this universal mystery of the divine incarnation Saint Gregory of Nyssa would say that, "all of human nature became the Body of Christ with which He has been united".[7]

These concise ecclesiological observations in no way dispute or diminish the belief that Orthodoxy is "the one, holy, catholic and apostolic Church". These comments simply underline her responsibility to make her universality known, and also to sincerely take on her responsibility to show the world that "the life that was manifested, and we have seen, and bear witness, and declare to you that eternal life which was with the Father, and was manifested to us" (1 John. 1:2). The manifestation of life in Christ requires the Orthodox Church to transcend all introversion and with her theology, missionary and social work to show the treasure we have "in earthen vessels" (2 Cor. 4:7).

Jesus Christ Manifests the Tri-Hypostatic God to the World

In the Orthodox Tradition, the Person of Jesus Christ "is all, and in all" (Col. 3:11). As Saint Symeon the New Theologian has said, "Christ is the very beginning, the middle and the end; He who is in the first is in everything, and as He is in the first so He is in the middle and at the end . . . Christ is all things in all."[8] The Church is incomprehensible, when cut off from Christ or placed parallel to Him. There is such a connection of Christ and the Church, that, as Saint Gregory of Nyssa puts it, "looking towards this new world of the creation of the Church one sees within it Him who is all and in all".[9] Christ is, as Saint Gregory of Nyssa again says, "the true leader of the Church who gathers what is dispersed into one body, and those much led astray by various deceptions are assembled into one gathering".[10] For this reason "the Church is often called Christ by Paul".[11]

The unity of Christ and the Church is underlined through the sacraments as unique *theanthropic* communion, that is, as life that is both of God and of human beings. God came down to human beings in order to raise them to God. Saint John Chrysostom links or almost identifies the human flesh of Christ with the humanity of the Church. The Son of God incarnate "took on the flesh of the Church".[12] The body assumed by Christ is, according to Saint Athanasius the Great, "the original state of the Church". The body that the Son of God assumed, when He became man, is the starting point and the foundation of the Church, and "through this grace people received the favour of being called gods and sons of God".[13]

The Son of God, with His saving dispensation (*oeconomia*) in the flesh became "a mediator of a better covenant" (Heb. 8:6), who traversed the ontological gap that divided the uncreated Triune God from created humanity. Thus, with the saving dispensation of the Son of God, of One of the Trinity, a new chapter in the history of the world began: God in Three persons was manifested to the world.

Christ speaks about this revelation with absolute clarity, especially in his prayer as High Priest. In this prayer Christ, addressing his Father, having first declared, "I have manifested thy name unto men" (John. 17:6), who, "Now have known that all things whatsoever thou hast given me are of thee" (John. 17:7), prays that the faithful remain faithful to the name of God the Father "that they may be one, as we are" (John. 17:11). The unity of the ecclesial body is something analogous to the unity of the divine Persons. In this prayer, Christ prays for his disciples, but not just for them, "but for them also which shall believe on me through their word" (John. 17:20). The prayer has a major and crucial theme, which concerns the faithful everywhere, of every race and every age. This theme is "that all may be one". This unity is not understood as an external agreement, but as an existential compassion, abolishing all division.

The unity of the faithful is communicated through the unity of the three divine Persons, and in this way alone is esteemed as a unique communion and harmony of existence. "As thou, Father, art in me, and I in thee, that they also may be one in us: that the world may believe that thou hast sent me. And the glory which thou gavest me I have given them; that they may be one, even as we are one: I in them, and thou in me" (John 17:21–23). The "glory" which God the Father gave His Son before all ages, and which the Son gave to His disciples, "that they may be one" does not denote an abstract concept, but is the Paraclete, the Spirit of truth. By "Christ's own glory", points out Gregory of Nyssa, "is meant the Holy Spirit, which he gave to his disciples by breathing upon them, for what is scattered cannot otherwise be united unless joined together by the Holy Spirit's unity".[14]

Thus, through the Holy Spirit, Christ transmits his life to the life of those who are capable of accepting him. The life of Christ, that is, Christ himself, can only become man's own through the Holy Spirit. "If any man have not the Spirit of Christ, he is none of his" (Rom. 8:9). The Spirit is glory, as Christ himself pointed out when he addressed his Father: "Glorify thou me with thine own self with the glory which I had with thee before the world was" (John 17:5). When Saint Gregory of Nyssa comments on this passage from John, he makes the following clarification: "The Logos is God, who has the glory of the Father. However, because he became flesh, in these latter days, it was necessary for the flesh to become what the Logos always was (that is, divine) by uniting itself to it. This was actually realized when the flesh received what the Logos had before the world was made. This is none other than the Holy Spirit, the same Holy Spirit which existed before all ages, together with the Father and with the Son".[15]

In the entire patristic tradition a Triadology which is not based on Christology and does not follow Christology is incomprehensible. Moreover, it is impossible to have a Christology that is not illumined by Pneumatology. The mystery of the Trinity was manifested to the world by the Son of God Incarnate. He defined the method of entering the Body of the Church and the precise actuality of Church communion when he ordered his disciples to "Go ye therefore, and teach all nations, baptizing them in the name of the Father, and of the Son, and of the Holy Ghost" (Matt. 28:19). Furthermore, we do not know the Son of God incarnate independently, like a reformer and innovator, with some philosophical or ethical notions; rather, we know Him through the Holy Spirit. "No man can say that Jesus is the Lord, but by the Holy Ghost" (1 Cor. 12:3). The point is that the

incarnation of the only-begotten Son of God manifested and
revealed to human persons the mystery of the Trinity, upon which
all devotion and theology is based. The manifested communion
of the Trinity gave man the measure and foundation of his new
existence and his relationship with other persons. The revelation of God in Trinity is for the Church the first and preeminent
truth upon which is established the truth for human beings and
the miracle of unity of human persons in Christ.

*The Unity and Communion of the Church in the Image of the Unity and
Communion of the Holy Trinity*

IT is worth pointing out that in Christ's prayer as High Priest, by
which the God-Man reveals the mystery of the Trinity, there is
constant reference to unity. The word "one" is repeated several
times in just a few verses. It is also characteristic that the unity
of the Church is always understood in relation to the unity of the
Holy Trinity. Church unity is incomprehensible outside of its basis
in the Trinity. The unity of the Church is not based, as we have
already pointed out, on external, human and social elements, but
it is an outpouring of the unique and perfect harmony and unity
of the Divine Trinity. Pseudo-Dionysius points out that the Triune
God "brings everything together into unity without confusion,
into an undivided communion . . . This one simple nature . . . joins
all things to itself and to each other, preserving them in their
distinctiveness and yet linking them together in a universal and
unconfused alliance".[16]

   In other words, Church unity is not understood as autonomous, as exclusive in itself, but rather as a continuous, vital and
dynamic participation in the united divine life. Or, to put it another
way, the unity of the Holy Trinity transforms the human individualistic multiplicity into a harmonious concord and symbiosis.
Divine unity embraces every aspect of life within the Church,
"for as we have many members in one body, and all members have
not the same office: So we, being many, are one body in Christ,
and every one members one of another" (Rom. 12:4–5). This
internal unity of the Body of the Church, this unity in Christ and

through Christ, according to the image of the Trinity, is included in every aspect of life in the Church, and is shown in various ways in patristic tradition. As a typical example I refer to what Saint Ignatius the God-bearer said to the Philadelphians:

I exhort you to have but one faith, and one preaching, and one Eucharist. For there is one flesh of the Lord Jesus Christ, and his blood that was shed for us is one. One loaf also is broken for all, and one cup is distributed among them all. There is but one altar for the whole Church, and one bishop, with the presbytery and the deacons. Since also there is one unbegotten being, God the Father, and one only-begotten Son, God the Word and man, and one Comforter, the Spirit of truth, and also one preaching, and one faith, and one baptism, and one Church which the Holy Apostles established from one end of the earth to the other with the Holy Blood of Christ, and by their own sweat and toil, it behoves you also, therefore, as a 'peculiar people and a holy nation' to perform all things with harmony in Christ.[17]

From this picture given by Saint Ignatius we realize that the unity of the people of God is only possible through divine union. The council of the people of God in a new assembly is a communion in the image of the Trinity's communion. This new communion became possible only because the Son of God, freely transcending the bounds of biological life, created a new relationship between his uncreated being and created man. In the pre-Christian era the relationship between God and man was that between subject and object: God acted as a subject from without, behind the veil of history. "Hear this, all ye people; give ear, all ye inhabitants of the world" (Ps. 49:1 [LXX 48:2]). Thus, the unity of human persons was a result of submission to the voice, the commandments of God, to an external law. In the reality of the new people unity is a result of cohabitation and indwelling; it is a result of the fact that God the Word himself "was made flesh, and dwelt among us" (John 1:14). The new reality of the Church is no longer determined by a subject–object relationship, but by the taking on of creation and its participation in what is uncreated. By his unique *kenotic* act the Son of God completely transforms the subject–object relationship. He gives another meaning and another dynamic to the relationship between God and man. Here, human history is not a field of action viewed from above by a judging and law-giving God. Rather, it is the space that God takes on, who enters history with his incarnation. The Son of God through his incarnation became history, and gave history new meaning.

Pseudo-Dionysius and Saint Maximus the Confessor, in their attempt to understand the relationship between divine unity and the unity of the people, speak of the *ecstasy* of God, of the movement of God in order to meet the human person. The Son of God's *ecstasy* is a movement towards an encounter, an exodus of God and an indwelling in the reality of human existence. This *ecstasy* of God is joined with love. "Thus, the Incarnation implies an exodus of God out of himself, while he yet stays within himself, in order to eliminate the existing gulf between God and man. This ecstasy or movement of God is understood in terms of divine love. 'For God so loved the world, that he gave his only begotten Son' (John. 3:16)."[18]

Thus, the Person of the Son of God incarnate became the cause of Church unity. Just as the Person of God the Father, who generated the Son eternally and again made the Spirit proceed eternally, is the only cause of existence of the other two divine Persons, and in this way established the unique communion of the Trinity, in the same way Christ established the communion of the Church. Just as the Father is the ontological, so to speak, basis of communion of the Trinity, in the same way the Son is the ontological basis of the communion of the Church, which is according to the image of the communion of the Trinity.

We can further develop this idea. With the incarnation of the Son of God and with the free acceptance of the gifts of the incarnation on the part of the believer, through baptism, man is again raised to personhood. Through baptism the obscured divine image is restored in man. Whatever was left in human nature by sin, that is, alienation and self-centredness, is cured and the human person can commune with God and his fellow human being again. In the whole of Church tradition sin has been understood as disintegration, rupture, dilution, as the breakup of the original unity, which God determined as man's way of existence and life. Thus, man was separated from God, was separated from his fellow human person, and there was even a rift in his very own being, a violent rupture of his coherence. It was what is known in the psychiatric terminology as schizophrenia or split personality. Thus, through sin, the human person lost the purity that God gave him at creation. Man returns to this original condition with his entrance into the Church, where he can again partake of God and commune with his fellow men, and live in inner coherence and equilibrium. So, the restoration of the image in each human person through baptism also brings about the restoration of human communion, in the image of the Triune communion. This is in fact the Church, communion and unity not simply of "units" – individuals – but communion, unity and coexistence of persons.

The Image of the Trinity and the Hierarchical Order of the Church

PSEUDO-DIONYSIUS, in his work *On the Ecclesiatical Hierarchy,* refers to the Trinitarian source of Church unity, and how this is transmitted as life which guarantees the harmony of the ecclesial body. The hierarchical structure of the Church was never understood in the East as an administrative device, but first and foremost as a ministry of vital importance for the existence and stability of the ecclesial body. Hierarchical responsibility in the East was always a ministry of unity and sanctification of the body of the Church.

The source of this hierarchy is the font of life, the being of goodness, the one cause of everything, namely, the Trinity which in goodness bestows being and well-being on everything . . . The common goal of every hierarchy consists of the continuous love of God and of things divine, a love which is sacredly worked out in an inspired and unique way, and before this, the complete and unswerving avoidance of everything contrary to it. It consists of a knowledge of beings as they really are. It consists of both the seeing and the understanding of sacred truth. It consists of an inspired participation in the one-like perfection and in the one itself, as far as possible. It consists of a feast upon that sacred vision which nourishes the intellect and which divinizes everything rising up to it.[19]

The ecclesial hierarchy and Christian priesthood, in general, was understood in Eastern Christendom as an example of the continuous presence, through the Holy Spirit, of Christ in history. The important role of the bishop and the priest and their work in the preservation and expansion of the unity of the ecclesial body is based on the Christological and Pneumatological character of this ministry. It is noteworthy that this link between priesthood and the ministry of Christ is mentioned in the New Testament. While the old priesthood could not save man, with the priesthood of Christ a new condition begins. "By that will we have been sanctified by the offering of the body of Jesus Christ once for all. And every priest standeth daily ministering and offering repeatedly the same sacrifices, which can never take away sins. But this man, after he had offered one sacrifice for sins for ever, sat down at the right hand of God, from that time waiting till his enemies be made his footstool. For by one offering he hath perfected for ever them that are being sanctified" (Heb. 10:10–14).

In Church tradition it is fundamental that Christ is the "firstborn" and "Archpriest", the "eternal priest" from whose power the Apostles and those who followed them gained the gift of priesthood, and thus the whole earth was filled with glory and grace.[20] The Christological and Pneumatological character of priesthood co-exist in harmony. Christian priesthood actually calls for participation in the priesthood of Christ. The descent of the Holy Spirit upon the newly ordained priest is what establishes this participation. This means that the person being ordained has a direct link with the priesthood of Christ, which is achieved with the descent of the Holy Spirit.[21]

When we associate priesthood with the Person of Christ and with the advent of the Holy Spirit, in essence we associate it with One God in Three Hypostases. In patristic theology, Christology and Pneumatology are always placed within the framework of Trinitology. Saint Maximus would say that "true priesthood is actually a figure in all respects of blessed divinity".[22] Before this Saint Ignatius would exhort the faithful and at the same time say: "Let all men respect the deacons as Jesus Christ, and the bishop as being a type of the Father, and the presbyters as the council of God and as an association of Apostles, without this it cannot be called a Church."[23] In a spurious work attributed to Athanasius there is a dialogue between an Orthodox Christian and an anonymous heretic. Here, the following is mentioned:

"The bishop, the presbyter and the deacon are like the Father, the Son and the Holy Spirit".[24] We find a similar typology in the liturgical works of Saint Symeon of Thessalonica. Here, Christian priesthood is referred to as "divine", a concept which we also find earlier in Saint Gregory of Nyssa, who calls it a "divine matter".[25] Saint Symeon of Thessalonica, following the Areopagitical works says that: "in the type of the Trinity we have these three: the deacon, the presbyter and the bishop".[26]

Thus, the ecclesial hierarchy and the priesthood, in general, remain in the Church as a ceaseless charismatic reminder that the ecclesial body is, in the image of the communion of the Trinity, a communion of persons, united by common faith and life. This common life of love starts with Baptism, the act of restoring the human person, and continues with the Divine Eucharist, with the sacrament of communion of persons. In her eucharistic assembly, especially, the Church confirms that she exists as a communion with God the Father in Christ and the Holy Spirit. She confirms that she already lives in the blessed kingdom of God, as shown by the declaration of the priest at the beginning of the Divine Liturgy: "Blessed is the kingdom of the Father, and of the Son, and of the Holy Spirit". The bread and wine of communion constitute the central point of Church unity, "of the assembly into the One, that is, God".[27] The Eucharist is the historical realization of the words of Christ to God the Father: "I in them, and thou in me, that they may be made perfect in one; and that the world may know that thou hast sent me, and hast loved them, as thou hast loved me. Father, I will that they also, whom thou hast given me, be with me where I am; that they may behold my glory, which thou hast given me: for thou lovedst me before the foundation of the world. O righteous Father, the world hath not known thee: but I have known thee, and these have known that thou hast sent me. And I have declared unto them thy name, and will declare it: that the love wherewith thou hast loved me may be in them, and I in them" (John 17:23–26).

The responsibility of Orthodoxy today is to prove with her attitude and works that she continues to exist as a communion of persons and local Churches in the image of the Trinity's communion. She must show the world, with her obedience to the Gospel and patristic tradition, with her dedication to the decisions of the Ecumenical Councils and her Church canons, that she is a creation of God in Trinity and a reflection of the glory of the Father, and of the Son, and of the Holy Spirit.

NOTES

* Paper presented to the International Conference of the Theological Commission of the Moscow Patriarchate, held in Moscow, from November 17 to 20, 2003.

1. *On Psalms* 23 (PG 12:1265B).

2. *Definition of Faith*, Fourth Ecumenical Council (451).

3. *Octoechos*, First Tone, Saturday evening vespers, *aposticha.*

4. *Homily on the Cross and on the Thief* 1 (PG 49:401).

5. "The universality of salvation in Christ", Θεολογία 51 (1980), pp. 655–656.

6. Archimandrite Sophrony Sakharov, *Saint Silouan the Athonite* (Essex, 1991), pp. 63–65

7. *When all things shall be subdued unto him*, ed. J. K. Downing, p. 21, 10–11; PG 44:1320B.

8. *Practical and Theological Chapters* III, 1; trans. P. McGuckin (Kalamazoo MI, 1982), p. 72: revised.

9. *On the Song of Songs* 13, ed. H. Landerbeck, p. 386, 4–7; PG 44:1052A.

10. *Homilies on Ecclesiastes* 1, ed. P. Alexander, p. 280, 8–11; PG 44:620B.

11. *Life of Moses* II, ed. H. Musurillo, p. 95, 12–13; PG 44:385A.

12. *Homily Before His Exile* 2 (PC 52:429).

13. *On the Incarnation and Against the Arians* 12 (PG 26:1004B).

14. *When all things shall be subdued unto him, op. cit.,* p. 21, 22–23; PG 44:1320CD).

15. *When all things shall be subdued unto him, op. cit.,* pp. 21, 22–23, 16; PG 44:1320D–1321A. See also, *Against the Macenonians*, ed. F. Müller, pp. 108, 30–109, 15; PG 45:1329AB; *On the Song of Songs* 15, *op. cit.,* pp. 466, 14–467, 17; PG 44:1116D–1117B; and my article, "The People of God. Its Unity and Its Glory: A discussion of John 17:17–24 in the Light of Patristic

Thought", *The Greek Orthodox Theological Review* 30 (1985), 419 [reprinted in the present edition].

16. *On the Divine Names* 11 (PG 3:949C).

17. *To the Philadelphians* 4; see also 1 Peter 2:9.

18. C. Scouteris, "The People of God", *op. cit.*, p. 403.

19. *Ecclesiastical Hierarchy* 3 (PG 3:373C–376A). Quotation taken from C. Luibheid's English translation, *Pseudo-Dionysius: The Complete Works*, Classics of Western Spirituality (New York, 1987), pp. 197–198.

20. Justin Martyr, *Dialogue* 42, 1: "... ἀπὸ τῆς δυνάμεως τοῦ αἰωνίου ἱερέως Χριστοῦ".

21. Scouteris, "Christian Priesthood and Ecclesial Unity: Some Theological and Canonical Considerations", *Kanon* 13 (1996), 137 [reprinted in the present edition].

22. *Letter to Bishop John* (PG 91:625A).

23. *To the Trallians* 3, 1.

24. *Dialogue on the Holy Trinity* 27 (PG 28:1156 ff).

25. *Life of Moses* II, *op. cit.*, p. 130, 15–16; PG 44:417B.

26. *On Holy Ordinations* (PG 155:364A).

27. *Ecclesiastical Hierarchy* 2, *op. cit.*, p. 209; (PG 3:424D).

Doxology
THE LANGUAGE OF THE CHURCH*

FOR A NUMBER OF YEARS great emphasis has been placed on the issue of theology. Its nature, task, method, and language have been a matter of study, explanation, investigation, and exploration by a great number of scholars, both Orthodox and those of other Christian traditions.[1] Although this can be viewed as positive from one vantage point, from another it reveals that, at the present time, theology is often in a condition of crisis and, to a certain extent, confusion. Our contemporary theologizing is quite often characterized either by a sense of self-sufficiency or artificial openness, the former manifesting itself in a mere repetition, a sort of conservative attachment to the past, the latter taking the form of a kind of modern, abstract, religious speculation. No sensitive observer will deny that in our theological scene there often exists a gulf between the so-called "academic" theological community and the ecclesiastical pastoral concerns of those responsible for the spiritual welfare of the people of God. Theological work and pastoral responsibility are very often scandalously treated as two different tasks.

It is certainly not my desire to be either skeptical or negative at such a gathering as the Third International Conference of Orthodox Theological Schools. However, it seems to me essential that reality be faced in order not to build castles in the sky. In order that our investigation be honest, clear, and constructive, it is of paramount importance to realize where we stand and what we represent.

The initial question concerning the theme for discussion should be posed as follows: What is the significance of "doxology, the language of Orthodoxy", in our modern age? What does doxology mean in our contemporary reality? The point being, do we have a clear enough vision to understand what doxological theology is in an era when our minds have been, to a great extent, obscured, and our theological and ecclesiastical consciences too often secularized or confused? The question demands an answer in terms of serenity, sincerity, frankness, and clarity.

From the patristic point of view, "doxology" is the essence of Christian life. Our subject, therefore, becomes vital and essential, demanding careful consideration and full attention. We are not discussing a matter for pure contemplation, a philosophical problem. Nor are we discussing a question of dialectic, not even a simple way of theologizing. We are, rather, discussing a reality directly connected with faith, love, and communion with him, from whom "every good endowment and every perfect gift" (Jas. 1:17) flow.[2] When we speak of doxology, we are obliged to touch upon the heart, the very being, of Christian understanding and of Christian life itself. Indeed, when we speak of "doxology", we stand very much at the centre of Orthodox theology.

Before proceeding to a discussion of the subject at hand, it would be appropriate to examine the terms "doxology", "theology", and "orthodoxy". In fact, the meaning of these three terms, in the writings of the Greek Fathers, interpenetrate one another, and the terms are often used interchangeably. Doxology is "the word (λόγος) about glory." But glory, in the final analysis, is God himself; the "unmoved glory" (ἡ ἀκίνητος δόξα), in the words of Saint John Chrysostom.[3]

God is the absolute glory, "glory and perfection itself" (αὐτοδεδοξασμένος καὶ αὐτοτέλειος), according to Saint Epiphanius.[4] In this sense, the terms doxology and theology describe the same reality. Doxology is the λόγος about glory (that is, about God). Doxology and theology are, therefore, identical. This identification was fully expressed by Origen when speaking of prayer. Thus, commenting on Matt. 6:7, he exhorts Christians not to "use vain repetitions", but to theologize, that is,, to ascribe glory to God.[5] Moreover, it is well known that this is not the only instance where Origen uses the term "theologize" to indicate the glorification of God. In several of his writings, both the terms theology and doxology are used interchangeably and as equivalents.[6] From Origen on, especially in the so-called ascetical tradition, identification of theology and doxology become more self-conscious and obvious. The well-known words of Evagrius constitute a summary: "If you are a theologian, you will pray in truth; and if you pray in truth, you are a theologian."[7]

On the other hand, the term "orthodoxy" indicates not merely right opinion or belief as opposed to heresy, but also right glorification; more accurately, right glorification encompassing right belief and a right way of expressing it. Thus, right doxology or, simply, doxology is a more comprehensive definition than right belief.

We may add in this connection that, according to Orthodox understanding, doctrinal tradition is not exclusively an intellectual system. Rather, it is inextricably bound together with liturgical action. It is within the worshipping community, and in light of the community's liturgical life, that doctrine becomes "a field of vision wherein all things on earth are seen in their relation to the things of heaven."[8]

In this respect, the *lex orandi* becomes the focus of the *lex credendi*, of the *lex cognoscendi*, and of the *lex vivendi*. Dogmas, in other words, are not abstract speculations in and of themselves. Likewise, Christian life is not moralistic and external behaviour based on regulations and laws. Both doctrine and the Christian way of life are understood within the liturgical context. Within the worshipping community, doctrine becomes that action which constitutes the highest point of the Christian way. Thus, the Orthodox approach both to doctrine and the Christian life is fundamentally a liturgical one.

For an Orthodox, it is self-evident that theology, as God's doxology, has not the characteristics of an individual, monistic dialogue between the theologizing person and God; but, although personhood remains its *locus,* it is an ecclesial offering. The theologizing person apprehends, in his theology, the mind of the ecclesial body and offers it to God; his own from his own, in a unique and personal way. I believe that it is this ecclesial conscience of theology that we express in our Liturgy when, immediately before our confession of common faith in the triune God, the Creed, we urge: "Let us love one another that with one mind we may confess the Father, the Son, and the Holy Spirit."[9] The one and only rock upon which theology as a doxological event can be based is the ecclesiastical body. It is within the Church, this continued Pentecost, that our mind, which is very often deprived of any orientation toward God, can be reoriented toward him, and, indeed, be illuminated and transformed into a theological mind. Moreover, it is only within ecclesial reality that the transfiguration of the human person can be accomplished. The Church herself is not a secular community, but "the tabernacle of God", which, in spite of the fact that she is here and now, transcends time and space and belongs to the "age to come"; the point being, that the ecclesial community is "gathered together" by the Holy Spirit. It is the "other Paraclete", he who maintains the ecclesial oneness, who thus secures solid ground for a genuine theological offering. It is he who transforms, within the Church, simple human persons into "theologians."[10] It is he only "by whom we cry out, Abba, Father" (Rom. 8:15). In fact, when we speak of doxology we mean an action of the Spirit, "for we know not what we should pray for as we ought: but the Spirit himself makes intercession for us with groanings which cannot be uttered" (Rom. 8:26).

The Question of Language

THEOLOGY as doxology, prayer, and orthodoxy of necessity employs the medium of language. In fact, it is an act carried out by language. When we speak of language in this context, we do not necessarily restrict it to the narrow limits of the created and spoken word. Expressed words do, indeed, represent part of theological language, but not its totality, and certainly not its highest part. I would venture to say that expressed words correspond to a minimum of theological language, which, in its essential part, transcends words and expressions.

My intention here is not to introduce a sharp distinction between the expressed and "inexpressible" word. On the contrary, I intend to underline the fact that language, both as an expression of divine truths (προφορικὸς λόγος), as well as an inward, immanent event (ἐνδιάθετος λόγος) is a unique reality and constitutes an essential element of theology.

The fact that there exists an inexpressible theological language has already been recognized by the well-known philosopher of language Ludwig Wittgenstein. Wittgenstein speaks specifically of the peculiarity of religious language. In his *Tractatus logico-philosophicus*, Wittgenstein recognizes that there are truths of religion which "cannot be put into words" (*Unaussprechliches*). For such truths we must remain silent. Silence here means that for religion and ethics we cannot always use "propositions" as we do for the natural sciences. From this perspective, religious language is to a great extent a distortion of language. Yet it is precisely through this distortion that religious truths become evident.[11]

In spite of the fact that in Wittgenstein's approach there is room to express through language what is known as mystical experience, there is still a substantial difference between his philosophy of language and its biblical, patristic understanding. Besides, by Wittgenstein's inability to explain how the mystical can be made evident, we observe that his entire system is based on an absolutely anthropocentric structure. The experience of God and the word about him are exclusively based on man and confined within the boundaries of human possibilities. In his theory of language there is absolutely no room for an experience which transcends human effort and ability; an experience such as that of Saint Paul who "was caught up to the third heaven . . . and heard inexpressible words" (2 Cor. 12:2–4).

Wittgenstein can easily accept a language of faith, or even a religious language, that expresses something transcending all human learning which is carried out by language; but in his philosophy there is no place for language which is given to men as grace.[12] The fundamental truth pointed out by Paul that, "the Spirit himself maketh intercession for us with groanings which cannot be uttered" (Rom. 8:26), remains something absolutely foreign, paradoxical, and even scandalous to human understanding.

In order to reach a better understanding of what language represents, from a biblical and patristic point of view, it is, I think, necessary to explain this issue further. According to Orthodox understanding, all processes concerning the communication of divine truths are closely interwoven. Speech, contemplation, and even communion with God through mystical experience, constitute an indivisible unity. This unity is summarized, to a great extent, in the term "logos" (word). This term, a Greek term *par excellence,* is "multi-sensed". As an expressed word, both oral and written, it can be viewed as a composition of words and phrases which become the means by which men understand one another. On the theological level, the expressed word is the way of transmitting transmittable divine truths which can be transmitted by created words. For logos as inward, immanent power is understood as contemplation. Logos as contemplation about God excels logos as expression of him. Such has already been said by Plato and repeated, in one way or another, by certain of the Greek Fathers.[13] The point being that although it is hard to form an adequate concept of God, it is even harder to express it. Thus, logos as contemplation has wider possibilities than logos as expression, whereas logos as truth excels both contemplation and expression. Logos as truth is the Divine Logos, who "became flesh and dwelt among us, and we beheld his glory, glory as of the Only-begotten of the Father, full of grace and truth" (John 1:14).

Thus, the Greek term "logos" was adopted by Saint John the Theologian and thereafter by the entire Christian tradition to designate the Son, the second person of the one and undivided Trinity, he who alone "knows the Father" (John 10:15) and reveals him "to whom he wills" (Matt. 11:27). The incarnation of the eternal Logos of God has, therefore, given new and unique perspective to theology. Through the self-emptying of the divine Logos the eternal truth of God was transmitted to men and expressed within the narrow limits of human language. The incarnate Logos spoke to man about God in a human way (ἀνθρωπίνως). He did so using words, images, parables, and concepts, in order that men might be able to speak of God in a way worthy of Him (θεοπρεπῶς).[14]

Origen comments that the Son of God is called Logos because that which is rational, and indeed, endowed with reason, is revealed in his person. He is called Logos because it is he who has transformed our life, one devoid of reason (πᾶν ἄλογον ἡμῶν), into a new reality and made us truly rational (κατὰ ἀλήθειαν λογικούς). Thus, "Whether . . . ye eat, or drink, or whatsoever ye do, do all to the glory of God" (1 Cor. 10:31). In other words, through his incarnation the Divine Logos gives us the possibility to be partakers of himself. As such, partaking of the life of the divine Logos constitutes restoration of our original reasonable life. Through participation in the life of the Logos man's life assimilates into the life of God. In Christ man's life becomes a risen life; his mind is elevated to the level of divine rationality.[15] This means that his mind is delivered from every dissolution and disorientation. Moreover, as far as he is a partaker of Christ, his theological language is not merely a human word, but takes on all the strength of the divine Word.[16]

I should at this point, in order to avoid any misunderstanding, make clear that theology as an ecclesial function, in its doxological dimension, is not the exclusive province of a certain elite enclave of specialists. On the contrary, it is an open *diakonia,* a reality of catholic significance. Even though theology is not limited to a certain minority of intellectuals, however, it is not one of the easiest things to do. Saint Gregory of Nyssa refers to theology as a mountain which is difficult to reach.[17] Saint Gregory the Theologian pays more attention to the preparation and presuppositions of theology. I would like to address only one of these points. In order to answer the question, "How can one theologize?" Saint Gregory speaks of, among other things, inner calmness (σχολή) and spiritual silence.[18] Silence, as a necessary method leading to theology, was also explicitly stressed by Saint Antony, the desert teacher. "In silence", he says in his *Texts of Saintly Life*, "you use your mind, and in using your mind you speak inwardly in yourself; for in silence mind gives birth to word. And a grateful word offered to God is salvation to man."[19]

We must admit that in our theological environment we do not often refer to silence. Our theological education overemphasizes the significance of the spoken or written word. Public speaking and homiletics have become basic theological courses in our faculties. Stressed by the mentality of the societies in which we live, we continue to pay less attention to what Saint Gregory calls σχολή, inward calmness and silence. I would say that our theological education suffers from, what I would call, a "Demosthenic" syndrome or a "Demosthenic" complex.

According to a certain biographical tradition, Demosthenes, the greatest Athenian orator, as a young student of rhetoric tried to overcome his stammering and thus obtain fluent speech. He often went to the seaside where by facing the sea and placing a few stones in his mouth, he practised the art of speaking. Thus, Demosthenes forced himself to become a rhetor. Athenian society, not unlike our modern societies, could only accept "successful" people. I have a feeling that we, too, train and force our students to become "successful" preachers, orators, and teachers of theology. Certainly, this is good from one point of view, but do we really prepare them to appreciate silence? Do we clear for them the way which leads to inner quietness and calm? In the *Gerontikon* we read that, "It was said of Abba Agathon that for three years he lived with a stone in his mouth until he had learned to keep silence."[20] Demosthenes and Agathon used the same method to attain diametrically different achievements. What, in fact, differentiates

Demosthenes from Agathon is the aim of their *ascesis*. The former intended to become an orator; the latter had in view, and earnestly desired, to learn to keep silence.

Glory and Glorification

WHEN we speak of silence, we do not suppose a pathetic, individualistic, and static condition, a kind of distortion of human personality. Silence is not a kind of consequence of anthropophobia. Rather, it is manifested in a deeply interior and spiritual quality. It is an existential, creative power, a healing and redirection of the whole man toward divine life. Silence is a profoundly Christian attitude, directly related to the divine *kenosis*. If we carefully study biblical data relating to the highest point of the abasement of the *Logos*, his passion and cross, we realize that Christ confronted his passion in absolute obedience and silence. In response to the question of the high priest: "Answerest thou nothing? . . . But Jesus was silent" (Matt. 26:62–63). Likewise, to the question of Pilate: "Answerest thou nothing? . . . But Jesus yet answered nothing" (Mark 15:4–5). Concerning his sacrifice on the cross, the prophecy of Isaiah certainly offers the most striking summary: "He was oppressed, and he was afflicted, yet he opened not his mouth: he is brought as a lamb to the slaughter, and as a sheep before her shearers is dumb, so he openeth not his mouth" (Isa. 53:7).

I emphasize the issue of silence because silence, not so much as a refusal to speak, but, primarily, as an attitude and as inward behaviour, is connected both to the glory of the incarnate *Logos* as well as to the possibility given to us to ascribe glory to God. In this respect we are confronted with the fundamental Christian paradox: silence, as an expression of the extreme self-emptying of the Word, and silence, as his glory, being bound together. It is precisely this paradox which is considered by the Jews a "scandal" and a "stumbling-block" (1 Cor. 1:23). For the Jews, the idea itself of the Lord of glory silent and crucified was not only unthinkable, but utter blasphemy. Moreover, according to the wisdom of the Greeks, the idea of a God humiliated, suffering in silence, and unable to succeed in showing his power, was far beyond any imagining, a real foolishness. However, that which is scandal to the Jews and foolishness to the Greeks, is, in the final count, "the power of God and the wisdom of God" (1 Cor. 1:24).

The fact to be clearly and definitely stressed is that the untreated and eternal glory of God, his power and wisdom, appeared to us through the abasement of God the *Logos*. This is what Saint John has clearly shown in his Gospel: "The Word became flesh and dwelt among us, and we beheld his glory, the glory as of the Only-begotten of the Father, full of grace and truth" (John 1:14). Glory has been transmitted to human reality because God, in his unique and ecstatic movement, has entered within the limitations of human poverty. He freely condescended to the human level in order that "we all, with unveiled face, beholding as in a mirror the glory of the Lord, are being transformed into the same image from glory to glory" (2 Cor. 3:18).

In the final analysis, the fact that the eternal glory of God appeared on the scene of human history, through the extreme humility of God the Logos, constitutes, indeed, the greatest paradox. For Greek society or our modern societies, which strive after progress and success and the acquisition of human glory and power, this is an indisputable contradiction; an open distortion of any law of this world. We as Christians often lack the inner capacity to understand that this contradiction and antinomy lead to truth and the "glorious liberty of the children of God" (Rom. 8:21). Our sight is not clear enough to see things as they really are rather than as they appear.

As a reminder, in this connection, Orthodox iconography personifies but one icon of Christ, entitled "the King of Glory." This unique icon is not an image of the Son of God in royalty and dominion, but rather, an icon of Christ exhausted and suffering. In his silent form as a servant, in extreme humility, lacking "beauty" and "form" (Isa. 53:2), in his mystery of the cross, the enhypostasized wisdom, glory, and power of God the Father revealed to us his glory, his divinity.

That which has been mentioned above, concerning silence and humility, is immediately applicable to the subject of doxology. Doxology is not vain verbalizing or triumphal words; it is, rather, the language of those who have denied themselves and lost their lives (Matt. 16:24–25). Doxology is indeed the language of those who have learned to keep silent. Thus, doxology is immediately connected with the life in Christ. It is the consequence of the life in Christ. In fact, doxology is the language of the saints and of all those who follow in the path of humility and obedience. To believe that there exists the possibility of putting forward a language of doxology without holiness is like believing that it is possible to put forward theology without God.

One has to be certain that, when speaking of "doxology as the language of Orthodoxy", Orthodox theologians, in fact, testify to their deep desire and existential agony to maintain and deepen the ethos, spirit and attitude of Orthodoxy. This, indeed, is our challenge and our mission.

NOTES

* Paper presented to the Third International Conference of Orthodox Theological schools, held in Brookline MA, from August 30 through September 4, 1987, and published in *The Greek Orthodox Theological Review* 38, nos. 1–4 (1993), 153–162.

1. Among other studies, we mention the following: N. A. Nissiotis, "La Theologie en tant que science et en tant que doxologie", *Irenikon* 23 (1960), 291; C. E. Papapetrou, *The Essence of Theology* (Athens, 1970) [in Greek]; C. B. Scouteris, *The Meaning of the Terms "Theology", "to Theologize", and "Theologian" in the Teaching of the Greek Fathers up to and Including the Cappadocians* (Athens, 1972) [in Greek]; A. Fermet and R. Marle, *Theologies d'aujourd'hui: J. Robinson, J. Ratzinger, H. Cox, H. Zahrnt, J. Moltman* (Paris, 1973); and E. L. Mascall, *Theology and the Gospel of Christ: An Essay in Reorientation* (London, 1977). See also the collective work, R. Vander Gucht and H. Vorgrimler, eds., *Bilan de la Theologie du XXe siecle* (Paris, 1970).

2. See also the "Prayer behind the Ambon", in the *Liturgy of Saint John Chrysostom*.

3. Saint John Chrysostom, *On the Epistle to the Romans* 3, 4 (PG 60:413).

4. Saint Epiphanius, *Against the Heresies* 69, 74 in K. Holl, ed., *Die Griechischen Christlichen Schriftsteller* (GCS), p. 222, 14–15; PG 42:321D.

5. Προσευχόμενοι μὴ βαττολογήσωμεν ἀλλὰ θεολογήσωμεν, Origen, *On Prayer,* in P. Koetschau, ed., GCS, p. 345, 3–4; PG 14:480C.

6. See for example: Origen, *On Jeremiah,* Hom. 18 in E. Klostermann, ed., GCS, p. 158, 9–15; PG 13:176A; *On Psalm* 67 in J. B. C. Pitra, ed., *Analecta Sacra Spicilegio Solesmeni Parata,* Vol. 3 (Paris, 1883), p. 80; *On Proverbs,* PG 13:24AB. For a further discussion of Origen's understanding of theology and doxology, see Scouteris, *The Meaning of the Terms "Theology", op. cit.,* pp. 81–85.

7. Evagrius, *On Prayer,* PG 79:1180B. V. Lossky referring to this passage of Evagrius reaches the conclusion that: "théologie gnose de la Trinité et oraison sont synonymes pour Évagre", *Vision de Dieu* (Neuchatel, 1969), p. 271.

8. G. Every, *The Byzantine Patriarchate* (London, 1947), p. ix. Quoted in T. Ware, *The Orthodox Church* (Harmondsworth, 1969), p. 271.

9. *The Liturgy of Saint John Chrysostom.*

10. This is explicitly pointed out in a hymn from the *Stichera* of Vespers for Pentecost: "The Holy Spirit provides everything; He overflows with prophecy; He fulfils the priests and has taught wisdom to the illiterate. He has elevated the fishermen to theologians. He gathered together the entire institution of the Church. O Comforter, consubstantial with the Father and the Son and sharing the same throne, glory to Thee."

11. See L. Wittgenstein, "Tractatus logico-philosophicus", in *Schrifften 1* (Frankfurt am Main, 1969), 6:42, 6:421, 6:45, 6:522. See also: H. O. Mounce, *Wittgenstein's Tractatus: An Introduction* (Oxford, 1981), pp. 99–100. C. Boudouris, *Wittgenstein's Theory of Meaning* (Athens, 1972), pp. 120–121 [in Greek].

12. This is a point which occurs in the teaching of the Fathers. See, for example, Didymus the Blind, *On the Holy Trinity* 3 (PG 39:825A); *On Psalms,* PG 39:1129A. Eusebius, *Ecclesiastical Theology* 1, 20, in Klostermann, GCS, p. 96, 7–10; PG 24:892C.

13. Plato, *Timaeus* 28c. See also Cyril of Alexandria, *On John* 14, 20 in P. E. Pusey, ed., p. 480; PG 74:237A. Saint Gregory the Theologian

56 Constantine Scouteris

changes the abovementioned phrase as follows: Θεὸν νοῆσαι χαλεπὸν·
φρᾶσαι δὲ ἀδύνατον, *Theological Oration* II, 4 (*Oration* 28), A J. Mason,
ed., p. 26; PG 36:29C.

14. Papapetrou, *The Essence of Theology, op. cit.,* p. 44.

15. Origen, *On John 1, 37,* in Klostermann, GCS, p. 47, 21–29; PG 14:96D:
Λόγος καλεῖται πᾶν ἄλογον ἡμῶν περιαιρῶν καὶ κατὰ ἀλήθειαν λογικοὺς
κατασκευάζων, πάντα εἰς δόξαν Θεοῦ πράττοντας μέχρι τοῦ ἐσθίειν καὶ
τοῦ πίνειν, εἰς δόξαν Θεοῦ ἐπιτελοῦντας διὰ τὸν λόγον καὶ τὰ κοινότερα
καὶ τὰ τελειότερα τοῦ βίου ἔργα. Εἰ γὰρ μετέχοντες αὐτοῦ ἀνιστάμεθα
καὶ φωτιζόμεθα, τάχα δὲ καὶ ποιμαινόμεθα ἢ βασιλευόμεθα, δῆλον
ὅτι καὶ ἐνθέως λογικοὶ γινόμεθα, τὰ ἐν ἡμῖν ἄλογα καὶ τὴν νεκρότητα
ἀφανίζοντος αὐτοῦ, καθ᾽ ὃ Λόγος ἐστὶ καὶ ἀνάστασις.

16. For a further discussion, see: Scouteris *The Meaning of the Terms
"Theology", op. cit.,* pp. 167 ff.

17. Ὅρος γάρ ἐστι ἄναντες ὡς ἀληθῶς καὶ δυσπρόσιτον ἡ θεολογία, ἧς
μόλις ὁ πολὺς λεὼς τὴν ὑπώρειαν φθάνει, Saint Gregory of Nyssa, *Life of
Moses,* H. Musurillo, ed., p. 84, 21–22; PG 44:373D-376A.

18. Δεῖ γὰρ τῷ ὄντι σχολάσαι καὶ γνῶναι Θεόν· καὶ ὅταν λάβωμεν καιρὸν
κρίνειν θεολογίας εὐθύτητα, Saint Gregory the Theologian, *Oration* 27, 3,
A. J. Mason, ed., p. 5, 6–8; PG 36:16A.

19. *The Sayings of the Desert Fathers,* trans. B. Ward (London, 1981), p. 22.

20. *Ibid.*

Church and Justification

ONE OF THE TRAGIC REALITIES OF MODERN man is the suffering which he often undergoes unjustly and that which he himself often unjustly inflicts upon others. Against this unhappy situation the Church comes to pit her very own being, her very own life: "For the life was manifested, and we have seen it, and bear witness, and shew unto you that eternal life, which was with the Father, and was manifested unto us" (1 John 1:2). Indeed, the entire gospel, the good news of the Church about this new life, could be summarized in the words of Saint John: "And the Word was made flesh, and dwelt among us" (John 1:14). Herein lies the truth about God and man. Here the fulfilment of revelation can be found, since revelation does not refer only to God but also to man. For an optimistic understanding of man, it is particularly important to realize that in the incarnation of the Logos not only are things concerning God revealed, but so too is the meaning of man's existence to its full extent. The dimension and the full potential of the human person were made evident in the *theandric* hypostasis of Christ, since, as Saint Athanasius says, "He became man so that we could be deified."[1]

In order to approach the entire issue of the justification of man, and to examine more specifically the relation between Church and justification, it is necessary to start from the christological basis. Moreover, it is well known that Orthodox theology cannot but use this starting point when referring to man. Within the patristic understanding no autonomous system of thought can be found regarding man, no anthropology in the narrow sense. The whole teaching of the Greek Fathers concerning man is, without a doubt, theology; or if you prefer, theological anthropology. The standard for understanding and judging man is not man himself, but the God-Man.

Thus, man's justification is to be seen in all its inscrutable fullness in the divine *kenosis*. Indeed, with the incarnation, not only are the results of man's fall rectified but also a new creation of man takes place. As Saint Gregory of Nyssa would say: "A new heaven is built, that is to say the steadfastness of the faith in Christ, and the earth is formed anew, and a different man is created."[2] Through the incarnation new perspectives, hitherto unknown, are opened to man; we are, indeed, faced with a recreation of man. Paul, when referring to the first and second Adam, attempts in a simple and figurative way to sketch the infinite potentialities of the New Testament man: "The first man is of the earth, earthy: the second man is the Lord from heaven. As is the earthy, such are they also that are earthy: and as is the heavenly, such are they also that are heavenly" (1 Cor. 15:47–48).

Through the incarnation, human nature does not simply receive divine gifts; it is not sealed only with the rich inpouring of divine grace, but is united hypostatically with God the Logos, and remains thereafter, in unity with him, "without confusion, without change, without division, without separation", always present in his divine hypostatis. In the incarnation human nature is united with the divine nature in a unique way, so as to surpass any other union and relationship, whereas at the same time "the difference of the natures is in no way destroyed on account of the union, but rather the peculiar property of each nature is preserved and concurring in one person and one hypostasis."[3]

The unity of the divine and human nature in the person or the hypostasis of God the Logos – this assumption of the entire human nature – constitutes the secret of man's redemption. Saint John of Damascus, summarizing the patristic teaching up to his time, declares explicitly: "He in his fullness took upon himself me in my fullness and was united whole to whole that he might in his grace bestow salvation on the whole man. For what has not been taken cannot be healed."[4] The incarnation of the Logos as the vivification and resurrection of the whole humanity can be seen in the unbroken unity constituted by human nature as underlined by many Greek Fathers, and more especially by Saint Gregory of Nyssa. Humanity forms a real and concrete unity, τὸ τῆς ἀνθρω-πότητος πλήρωμα. With great satisfaction Saint Gregory of Nyssa sees in the lost sheep of the evangelical parable the symbol of this single humanity reunited by the Good Shepherd to the "ninety-nine", the innumerable multitude of angels.[5] This unity of the human race forms the ontological basis for our incorporation into Christ and our redemption in him.[6] When Saint Gregory states that the "body of Christ is the whole human nature to which he was united",[7] he presupposes the unity of the human "lump" and wants to stress the universal character of salvation in Christ. The point is that when Christ, through the mercy and goodness of his Father, appeared to us in a human body, that is, when he had taken an individual and concrete human nature, he united to himself the whole human πλήρωμα, and by that union he redeemed, restored, perfected and transfigured it.

Starting with this universal dimension of the incarnation, we can easily understand where the basis of man's justification is to be placed. Justification is proper dignity in a way which is unique, perfect and complete. In this way "our life is hid with Christ in God" (Col. 3:3). It is particularly important to note that this central theme runs through the whole history of christological doctrine; in other words, the incarnation of the Logos is itself redemption, restoration, life, and justice.

What has been said so far shows, I think, that the incarnation of the Logos, as the manifestation of God, signifies the revealing of life and, consequently, the revealing of the authentic existence of man. Incarnation is the *kenosis* of God, which leads to the vivification of man. This *kenosis*–vivification begins, according to the apostolic teaching, with the birth of Christ and is completed with his death on the cross. God the Logos "made himself of no reputation, and took upon him the form of a servant, and was made in the likeness of men: and being found in fashion as a man, he humbled himself, and became obedient unto death, even the death of the cross" (Phil. 2:7–8). Thus, life is offered through death. Here lies the "foolishness" and the "scandal" of Christianity; the paradox of Christian faith: life through death, from voluntary death, to the glory of resurrection, to new life.

Let us dwell here, for a moment, on this issue of Christ's death.[8] First of all, it is necessary to stress that this paradoxical death is an act of supreme and complete obedience. To the disobedience of the first Adam which had death as its consequence, the second Adam juxtaposes his own total obedience: "He became obedient unto death." Whereas the disobedience of the first Adam had death as its result, the obedience of the second Adam opens the way for our vivification. Through Adam's decision to obey the promptings of the devil, because of his inability to use properly the gift of freedom, enmity arose between God and man. In the language of the New Testament, the term enmity does not mean hostility on God's part towards man, but expresses precisely the opposite: the enmity which fallen man feels towards God first, and then towards his fellow man. This enmity is the fatal fruit of the decision taken by man to place himself "at the east of the garden", that is, outside the dimension of the original communion of love between God and himself. In this sense, man exchanged his spiritual mind, which was the fruit of his real being, with the carnal mind, which is the result of his nonexistent earthly life. Saint Paul vividly describes the tragedy of man who finds himself in a state of enmity: "For to be carnally minded is death; but to be spiritually minded is life and peace. Because the carnal mind is enmity against God: for it is not subject to the law of God, neither indeed can be" (Rom. 8:6–7).

Through his death, Christ creates a new kind of relationship between God and man. "By the cross, having slain the enmity thereby" (Eph. 2:16), he accomplishes reconciliation: being "enemies, we were reconciled to God by the death of his Son" (Rom. 5:10). Death on the cross is the highest act of love towards man: "But God commendeth his love towards us, in that, while we were yet sinners, Christ died for us. Much more then, being now justified by his blood, we shall be saved from wrath through him. For if, when we were enemies, we were reconciled to God by the death of his Son, much more, being reconciled, we shall be saved by his life" (Rom. 5:8–10). Therefore, justification in the face of God is not gained through the endeavour and the achievements of man, but it comes as a gift of the grace of God to fallen man: "For all have sinned, and come short of the glory of God; Being justified by his grace through the redemption that is in Christ Jesus" (Rom. 3:23–24).

On this point we must make a necessary clarification: there is a difference between saying that God the Logos assumed the whole of human nature and that he "hath given himself for us an offering and a sacrifice" (Eph. 5:2). This "hath given himself" signifies that sin is removed by a voluntary offering. The state of sin is not dissolved with incarnation; in other words, redemption is not the automatic outcome of the union between divine and human nature; it is precisely the result of Christ's will. Christ is "the lamb of God, which taketh away the sin of the world" (John 1:29), not because the divine and human nature were hypostatically united in him, but because he freely chose the cross and death. This act of choice is a token of the love he had as man.

Moreover, it must be added that the passion and the cross have a wider meaning: the whole of Christ's life on earth was an unending passion, a suffering love for mankind. This we stress, in order to avoid the pitfall of fragmenting Christ's work, which inevitably leads to scholastic interpretations. The work of Christ has a fullness, and the redemption which derives from it is not related only to some isolated events of his earthly life. The whole course of the Saviour's life on earth forms a totality, an organic whole, from which it is not possible to separate and to isolate this part or the other. Of course, the final step to this unique course is death on the cross, as indeed Christ himself certified: "For this cause came I unto this hour" (John 12:27). But death on the cross is preceded by the suffering of a whole lifetime: the suffering for the enmity of man, for the isolation of the human person, for the "whole world" which "lieth in wickedness" (1 John 5:19).

Another point which must not escape our attention is that we cannot have a correct understanding of the mystery of Christ's death if we use moral or legalistic categories as our foundation. Christ's death was not the death of a righteous man, which could lead us to moral conclusions; nor was it a case of "settling accounts", or something necessary for the satisfaction of divine justice. Christ's death has another dimension because it was the death of that pure human nature which through its assumption into the hypostasis of God the Logos, had already been deified. We are dealing here with a unique death, with a death which is not the consequence of sin, and which precisely for this reason is the removal of sin.

Generally speaking, death is the separation of the soul from the body. And in the case of Christ's death the same holds true: his soul was separated from his body. But because the one hypostasis of the God-Man cannot be divided, even though his soul and body were so separated by death, they remain, nevertheless, united because of the divinity of the Logos from whom they cannot be estranged (hypostatic union). Christ's death is, therefore, death without corruption, and for this reason it constitutes the end of death. In other words, through this incorruptible death corruption itself and death are conquered. In essence, this death is the resurrection of human nature. And so, with this death the incarnate Logos "has blotted out the handwriting of ordinances that was against us, which was contrary to us, and took it out of the way, nailing it to his cross" (Col. 2:14).

Orthodox theology is content with this dogmatic statement, and consistently avoids moving on to analyses or scholastic interpretations. It is clear that in patristic thought the whole theology of the cross is free from legalities and scholastic elaborations. It is sufficient for the Greek Fathers to repeat the words of the New Testament and to describe, rather than determine or simplify with logical argumentations, the great mystery of godliness. They have no tendency for speculation, but restrict themselves to a doxological understanding of Christ's death. What we are faced with here is the mystery of God's love for mankind, through which all the consequences of the fall are nullified. These consequences would have been eternal if the incarnation of philanthropic economy had not transformed condemnation into justification by blotting out, not man himself, but the sin which did injustice to man.

But the death of Christ as the ultimate expression of his suffering love for mankind has no element of compulsion in it. Respect for man's freedom remains intact. In this way each man can find his justification by going through the mystery of death himself: "Know ye not, that so many of us as were baptized into Jesus Christ were baptized into his death? Therefore we are buried with him by baptism into death: that like as Christ was raised up from the dead by the glory of the Father, even so we also should walk in newness of life. For if we have been planted together in the likeness of his death, we shall be also in the likeness of his resurrection: Knowing this, that our old man is crucified with him, that the body of sin might be destroyed, that henceforth we should not serve sin. For he that is dead is freed from sin" (Rom. 6:3–7). In the Greek original, the "is freed from sin" of the authorized King James' version reads, δεδικαίωται ἀπὸ τῆς ἁμαρτίας, that is to say, "is justified from sin". And so, through baptism, which is an imitation of Christ's death and resurrection, man is justified: "He that is dead is *justified* from sin." With baptism man realizes in himself what Christ achieved by his voluntary death: Life from death. Individuals can be born in the new life of resurrection only if they die and are buried together with Christ through baptism.

In the Orthodox tradition, entering the Church is understood as the justification of man. If we want to express it in a clearer and more absolute way, justification is the Church. Inside the Church man finds his ancient authenticity. He is freed from the bondage of corruption and death and regains his original beauty, the glorious liberty of the children of God. Sin, which has done injustice to man, disappears and a new era of glory for man begins. The Son of God gives himself up (παραδίδει ἑαυτόν) for the forgiveness of sins and for the life of the world. Through the incarnation of the Logos, which is an abundance of love and offering, the Church enters a new era of glory: "Christ loved the Church, and gave himself for it; that he might sanctify and cleanse it with the washing of water by the word, That he might present it to himself a glorious Church, not having spot, or wrinkle, or any such thing; but that it should be holy and without blemish" (Eph. 5:25–27).

The entire reality of the Church is inseparably bound up with the mystery of death on the cross: Christ "gave himself *for* the Church". Man must first die through baptism in order to enter the Church. And after that, his membership in the Church must be an ongoing process of participation in the divine passion and death. Life always passes through death. Consequently, the death of the God-Man on the cross is not simply an historical event, an affair of the past; on the contrary, it covers every bit of the historical present of the life of the Church; it becomes the central point of the Church's life and unity. In this sense, the justification of the entire man, which materializes through Christ's death, has not only a moral, but primarily a sacramental significance. This objective fact is transferred into the personal life of every believer. Each one takes part in the Lord's Supper. In every eucharistic service and before receiving Communion, every Orthodox faithful prays: "At thy mystical supper, O Son of God, today receive me as a communicant; for I will not speak of the mystery to thine enemies, nor give thee a kiss like Judas; but like the thief I confess thee: remember me, O Lord, in thy Kingdom."

The sacramental significance of death on the cross is revealed at the Lord's Supper, when Christ said, while offering bread and wine to his disciples: "This is my body which is given for you", and

"This cup is the New Testament in my blood, which is shed for you" (Luke 22:19–20). These words mean nothing less than the giving over of the mystery of death on the cross to the body of the faithful. It is the possibility which is given to the members of the Church for continuous participation in the death and resurrection of Christ, in this Pascha of the New Testament. It is significant that the handing over of the bread of life and of the cup of the New Testament takes place *before* the sacrifice on the cross, precisely so that the philanthropic character of the offering may be stressed. As Gregory of Nyssa tells us: "Christ does not wait for the necessity arising from his betrayal, and the brigand attack of the Judaeans, and Pilate's illegal decision, so that their wickedness can become the principle and cause of man's common salvation; but he anticipates the attack through his economy, according to the ineffable secret manner of the divine dispensation which is invisible to men."[9] Thus the Lord's Supper is not a prefiguration or a symbolic, prophetic performance of Christ's death, but a real sacrament which was officiated by Christ, the High Priest of the New Testament. Similarly, the Holy Eucharist is not simply a symbolic remembrance of the Lord's Supper, but also a real sacrament. It is the remembrance of "the cross, the grave, the resurrection on the third day, the ascension into heaven, the enthronement at the right hand, and the second and glorious coming". However, apart from its "anamnestic" character, the Holy Eucharist, according to the Orthodox understanding, is an offering "in all and for all . . . for the holy catholic and apostolic Church".[10] It is the mystery of the presence, not fictitious or formal, but a real presence. In this way, through the Holy Eucharist, Christ's death and resurrection become a constant presence in the life of the Church. The mystery of death through the cross exists in the "here" and the "now" of the Church.

In the Eucharist man's death is assumed and transformed into life. Life is grafted onto death. It is, hence, a mystery of transfiguration. This assumption of man's sin and death and its transformation into a life of communion with God is precisely the new condition which is incarnated in the Church.

The eucharistic gathering is the restoration of the ancient communion between man and God. In it the true being of man is realized, since man really exists only when he is in communion with God. The eucharistic communion as a lifting of the division caused by the fall, and as a unification of life, is, in the final analysis, a creation of man after Christ's likeness, and for this reason his justification as well. Thus, man becomes, if we repeat Nicholas Cabasilas' way of putting it, a justice after Christ's likeness (δικαιοσύνη χριστοειδής).

We should at this point state that the unification of man's divided nature, which occurs in the Holy Eucharist, this justice after Christ's likeness, is not offered to man unconditionally. There is nothing magical or self-evident in the communion between God and man which takes place in the Eucharist. For the tree of justification to give fruit, there must exist the root of human justice. Cabasilas uses the biblical analogy of the wild olive tree: man is compared to a wild olive tree which left on its own is sterile and barren, that is, it is unable to bear fruits of justice. But when the good olive tree is grafted onto the wild olive tree it brings about a complete transformation. Thus, the fruits which come from the root of the wild olive tree are the fruits of a good olive tree. But for these fruits to exist, the root is necessary; in other words, man's personal effort and *ascesis* are required. Of course, this *ascesis* does not by itself lead to justification: good deeds alone do not bring merit, and likewise, faith alone does not restore man. Faith and deeds, that is, the results of man's *ascesis* are simply the preconditions. Faith and deeds form only the root of human justice, which when united to Christ's justice becomes justice after Christ's likeness.[12]

Orthodox theology has never ceased to underline the grace of God and the *synergy* (collaboration) of man. Man first receives the talent of God's gift and then adds his own personal work. Man's justification is basically an offering and an action of Christ; man, however, has a considerable degree of responsibility for the realization of justification. The field of action is open to man; he is free to create his own personal history of sanctification.

And thus we come to the chapter of *ascesis* and its significance for man's life. The Eastern Orthodox tradition considers
ascesis a fundamental reality. Orthodox spirituality and theology
are ascetical. Nothing of its life remains outside the dimension
of *ascesis*. The justification of man is the fruit of Christ's death
and resurrection. In baptism the believer passes through death,
in order to be resurrected, so that the new man, the enlightened
man, can be born. In the gathering of the Eucharist the Church
experiences Christ's death and resurrection continuously, as a
sacramental event. But death and resurrection are the two poles
between which moves man's entire spiritual course. Man must
die through *ascesis* so that he can live. He must become "dead
indeed unto sin, but alive unto God through Jesus Christ our
Lord" (Rom. 6:11).

The mortification of sin, this continuous death which is
achieved through ascetic training, opens for man the horizon
of understanding himself as eternal, and sets the foundation for
the revealing of the authentic human person. Here lies the basis
of holiness. *Ascesis* as a way of life, and not simply as practice of
certain specific methods or formal regulations, is the starting
point and the presupposition for the realization, within every
human "ego", of the life of justification, of sanctification, of deification. Through *ascesis* and sanctification Christ himself conveys
to man his own life, the life of passion and of resurrection; he
makes him, through the power of the Holy Spirit, the participant
of his uncreated divine energies, so that he can acquire the full
knowledge of his own personal immortality and eternity, and to
have the strength to abolish evil and every death and temptation,
since as Christ himself put it: "Verily, verily, I say unto you, He
that believeth on me, the works that I do shall he do also; and
greater works than these shall he do" (John 14:12). Through *ascesis*,
through this continuous personal passion, the life of the God-
Man Christ is placed upon the level of each individual believer.
Thus, not only the creation of justification, but its appropriation
is also the work of the God-Man.

The divine-human life of Christ is not something that belongs
to the past, a memory, a useful teaching, nor even a criterion for
the life of the present; this divine-human life exists, entirely, in the
theandric body of Christ, in the Church, and is being constantly
experienced by each one of its members, "in the measure of every
part". This *theandric* life was lived and is being lived through *ascesis*
by the saints. The life of the saints is in reality this very life of the
God-Man Christ. It is transferred from him to those who follow
him and is lived by them in his Church. On this point I should
clarify that I use here the term "saint" in a more dynamic and
broader, rather than a static and narrow, sense. Saints, inside the
Church, with prophetic powers, who can transmit the sense of
their eternity to the whole body of the faithful, are not only those
who due to their personal struggle and virtue were proclaimed
saints by the Church; but, also those who follow the life of saints,
that is, the life in Christ, and have "put off the old man, which is
corrupt according to the deceitful lusts" (Eph. 4:22).

According to Orthodox understanding, justification is incarnated in these persons. They have been justified through faith
and through deeds. They are those who have died, and who die
every day, and who for this reason are the sons of the resurrection. Going through death in every present instant of their life,
they become the bearers of the life of Christ, and hence they
transcend death. Within the Church, the saints are authentic
realities; "gods" by participation, who can teach in an unerring
manner, in a way which is incredibly stronger than myriads of
books, and who can even influence the life and faith of people
through their own life. The saints do not belong to themselves;
they belong to the Church, they are "catholic persons". They are
those who have surpassed themselves through *ascesis*, that is, those
who have elevated their *ego* to the level of the catholic *ego* of the
Church. They can, therefore, theologize with the theology of the
Church, and feel the pain of their fellow human beings through
the "feeling" (αἴσθησις) of the Church.

At this point, I must add one more clarification. In Western
theology we often see a distinction being made between justifi-

cation and sanctification. And one feels that we are dealing here
with two separate stages which are clearly distinguished from
each other. Justification is considered to be the first stage, the
starting point, after which follows the second stage, sanctification. I maintain that in Orthodox theology the matter is placed
on a different basis. What is stressed here is not the distinction between justification and sanctification, but the dynamic
character of justification. It is this very dynamism of justification which constitutes sanctification. Thus, man can become an
infinite being with immense potentialities opening before him.
Through baptism he puts on Christ; that is to say, he participates
in the justification which Christ himself created, while finding
the way open for him to raise himself "unto a perfect man, unto
the measure of the stature of the fullness of Christ" (Eph. 4:13).
Justification is a given fact, but at the same time it is a reality
towards which man continuously advances. It is, in the final
analysis, the process towards the unending end of perfection.

   Thus the saint, that is, the one in whom justification is manifest
in carrying on the divine-human life of Christ, becomes the heart
of the Church. He is a living testimony, a living "epistle" who can
teach the people of God. When Paul writes "unto the Church of
God which is at Corinth, with all the saints who are in all Achaia",
he says, "Ye are our epistle written in our hearts, known and read
by all men: Forasmuch as ye are manifestly declared to be an
epistle of Christ ministered by us, written not with ink, but with
the Spirit of the living God; not in tables of stone, but in fleshy
tables of the heart" (2 Cor. 3:2,3). In writing these words, Paul was
not using a verbal exaggeration, but desired to express the fact
that the saint, regardless of the time and period in which he may
live, is in reality "living and applied dogma", since he experiences
the eternal and saving dogmatic truths in all their life-giving and
creative power. In the person of the saint it becomes obvious, in
an absolute way, that dogmas are not just ontological truths in
themselves and for themselves, but that every dogma is a source
of life and spirituality; a truth pointed out by Christ himself: "the
words that I speak unto you, they are spirit, and they are life"

(John 6:63). Because the saint is himself a living doctrine, he is a kind of teacher and pedagogue within the Church. Because he himself continues the life of the God-Man Christ, that is to say, because he himself is the living manifestation of justification in every historic present of the Church's life, he can embrace the world. Through his grace he draws the world unto himself and sheds grace upon it.

Consequently, the subject 'Justification and Collective Faith' could be formulated in a more Orthodox theological manner as "The Saints and the Communion of Saints".

NOTES

* Paper presented at the International Colloquium held at Tantur Ecumenical Institute for Advanced Theological Studies, Jerusalem, in March 1982, and first published in *The Greek Orthodox Theological Review* 28, no. 2 (1983), 145-155.

1. *On the Incarnation of the Word,* ed. R. W. Thomson, p. 268; PG 25:192.

2. *On the Song of Songs* 13., ed. H. Langerbeck (Leiden, 1960), pp. 384–85 (PC 44:1049).

3. *Definition of Faith,* Fourth Ecumenical Council (451).

4. *Exact Exposition of the Orthodox Faith* 50. 35–37, ed. B. Kotter, pp. 151–52 (PC 45:1153).

5. *Against Apollinarius,* ed., F. Müller (Leiden, 1958), pp. 151–52; PG 45:1153.

6. See also my article, "Ἡ ἑνότης τῆς ἀνθρωπίνης φύσεως ὡς πραγματικὴ προϋπόθεσις τῆς σωτηρίας· ἐκ τῆς ἀνθρωπολογίας τοῦ ἁγίου Γρηγορίου τοῦ Νύσσης", *Θεολογία* 40 (1969), 416–429, and A. H. Armstrong, "Platonic Elements in Saint Gregory of Nyssa's Doctrine of Man", *Dominican Studies* 1 (1948), 113–126.

7. *When all things shall be subdued unto him,* in PG 44:1320B.

8. For a comprehensive discussion on Christ's death on the cross see, G. Florovsky, "Ὁ σταυρικὸς θάνατος" [Christ's Death on the Cross], *Ἀνατομία προβλημάτων τῆς πίστεως,* trans. M. Kalamaras (Thessalonica, 1977), pp. 52 ff.

9. *On Holy Pascha and on the Three-day Period of Christ's Resurrection,* PC 44:1320.

10. *The Divine Liturgy of Saint John Chrysostom.*
11. *The Life in Christ* (PG 150:592)
12. *Ibid.*

CHRISTIAN PRIESTHOOD AND ECCLESIAL UNITY
SOME THEOLOGICAL AND CANONICAL CONSIDERATIONS*

A T THE VERY BEGINNING OF THIS ADDRESS, I would like to say what a high honour and privilege it is for me to deliver the keynote lecture in this esteemed gathering of the Society for the Law of the Eastern Churches. My intention in this paper is to examine from a theological and canonical perspective the role of priesthood as an ecclesial ministry of unity.

1. THE records of the early Christian tradition leave no doubt that Christian priesthood is not a "function" necessary for the institutional being of the Church. Nor is it an autonomous, isolated and self-sufficient office belonging to the ordained individual. It is rather a ministry related and belonging to the entire ecclesial body. We can think of it as an *anaphoral* reality which is always in reference to and leads to the saving communion of the Body of Christ.

From the very outset of Christian history, priesthood was understood as a living testimony of the constant and continuing presence of Christ in every historic "now" of the life of the Church. It was viewed as a token of the Paschal fulfilment and *parousia*, bestowed to all Christians through the power of the

Holy Spirit. This means that priesthood was considered as an integral part of the ecclesial reality, related with and proceeding from the pentecostal economy.

In order to achieve a comprehensive understanding of the place of priesthood within the Christian community and to estimate its role for the ecclesial unity, it is important to stress its Christological and Pneumatological foundation. Any attempt to approach priesthood from a monistic point of view, that is as an autonomous subject, leads to divergent altered scholastic inter-pretations and speculations foreign to the Apostolic tradition.

Even a cursory study of the New Testament data reveals the fact that all titles related to ministry and priesthood are ascribed to Christ Himself. Christ is "apostle and high priest" (Heb. 3: 1); He is "priest" (Heb. 8: 4), "Teacher" and "Rabbi" (Matt. 23: 7–8); He is "a prophet . . . and more than a prophet" (Matt. 11: 9); He is "the Shepherd and Bishop of our souls" (1 Pet. 2: 25), "the Chief Shepherd" (1 Pet. 5: 4). Christ is "among us as the one who serves" (Luke 22: 27); He is the "diakonos" (Rom. 15: 8). In His priestly ministry Christ has "given Himself for us, an offering and a sacrifice to God for a sweetsmelling aroma" (Eph. 5: 2). In the New Testament Christ is both the victim and the priest who performs the sacrificing action. "We have been sanctified through the offering of the body of Jesus Christ once for all. And every priest stands ministering daily and offering repeatedly the same sacrifices, which can never take away sins. But this man, after He had offered one sacrifice for sins for ever, sat down at the right hand of God, from that time waiting till His enemies are made His footstool. For by one offering He has perfected for ever those who are being sanctified" (Heb. 10: 10–14).

In spite of the individual characteristics and significant differences in terms of perspective and style among such writers as Matthew, Paul, Peter and Luke, there is nothing more striking than the essential unity amid all diversity. This unity is basically that of a common attitude to Jesus Christ. There is among all New Testament authors a common sense that Christ "is the head of the body, the Church, Who is the beginning, the firstborn from the dead, that in all things He may have the pre-eminence" (Col. 1: 18).

Thus, from the authors of the New Testament themselves, from their understanding and conception of Christ, we can attest that Christian priesthood is directly related to Christ's ministry. The point is that priesthood is not simply a result of Christ's service in the world, not duplicate or parallel to it, but somehow is ontologically incorporated and identified with Christ's ministry. If the Church is Christ Himself extended into history, equally Christian priesthood is Christ's priestly office realized and extended in every historic period of the life of the Church. It is, so to speak, the reflection and the projection[1] of the saving work of Christ throughout the centuries. This means that priesthood is so inextricably bound up with the Person of Christ that our perception of the historical Jesus and of His ministry involves and determines our view of Christian priesthood.

At the heart of the early Christian tradition stands the belief that Jesus Christ is the "first-born" and the only Archpriest, according to the Father's nature.[2] The Apostles and those consecrated thereafter received the gift of priesthood "from the power of Christ, the eternal priest".[3] By asserting that priesthood is not to be regarded as an isolated, but as an event which must be taken in close connection with the fact itself of Christ, we mean that the primary content of priesthood is neither individualistic and functional, in the narrow sense of the term, nor moralistic, but essentially Christological.

2. THE Christological understanding of priesthood leads evidently to its Pneumatological foundation, given that "no one can say that Jesus is Lord except by the Holy Spirit" (1 Cor. 12: 3). In fact there is no way of understanding the Christological ground of priesthood other than by its Pneumatological dimension. It is only through the "economy of the Spirit" that we can approach the economy of the Son. The Holy Spirit was sent into the world through and in the name of the Son, in order to teach and bring to our remembrance all things that Christ performed for and said to us (John 14: 26).

It should be observed in this connection that, in relating priesthood to Christ's ministry, through the operation of the Holy Spirit, we do not propose either an exclusive Christology or an exclusive Pneumatology. The economy of the Son and the economy of the Spirit are not parallel, distinct, independent or self-determined divine actions. Theological autonomy does not correspond to orthodox Christology or Pneumatology. As the Son entered into the human reality "incarnate of the Holy Spirit and the Virgin Mary", so also the Holy Spirit comes into the world, being sent by the Son, to be an unceasing testimony of His work (John 15: 26), that is, to be a continuous historic possibility for the realization of Christ's ministry. Thus, through the Holy Spirit, Christ's priesthood remains present in the "here" and the "now" of ecclesial life. It is through the Holy Spirit that priesthood, in its historic manifestation, is related to Christ's priesthood. Christian priesthood and the priesthood of Christ belong together and should never be conceived individually apart, given that the Holy Spirit fills with His presence the Church and manifests Christ to all.

The Christological and the Pneumatological aspect of priesthood are present in a harmonious compound. They are inseparably blended together in a unique synthesis. The Christian priesthood involves the participation in Christ's own priestly mission. And it is precisely the personal descending of the Holy Spirit upon the newly-ordained that guarantees this participation. This means that the ordained person through the Holy Spirit is directly connected with the priesthood of Christ. The theandric *principium* of the priestly grace is pneumatologically present in the concrete ordained person. Through the *epiclesis* and coming of the Holy Spirit in ordination, the very priesthood of Christ is offered to the newly ordained, and remains alive and effectual within the ecclesial body. Thus the Holy Spirit, which was from the beginning with the Son, creating the cosmos, leading and inspiring the prophets, incarnating the eternal Logos of God in man, being always with Christ, raising Him from the dead, and constituting the Apostolic Church,[4] realizes Christ's own priesthood within the historic life of the Church. In other words, the Holy Spirit is and remains the vital link between Christ's priesthood and the Christian priesthood.

In considering priesthood in relation to Pneumatology, we are obliged to make special reference to the Pentecostal economy. It is well known that for the Church Pentecost is not simply a historic event, but rather a continuous and dynamic presence, an ever-flowing source of life. The late Fr. Georges Florovsky makes the observation that "Pentecost becomes eternal in the Apostolic Succession, that is in the uninterruptibility of hierarchial ordinations in which every part of the Church is at every moment organically united with the primary source".[5] Thus, through the ordained ministry the entire ecclesial body is related to the divine economy. Priesthood becomes an instrument for the realization of ecclesial communion, which is offered at every historic moment as continuous pentecostal life. In this perspective, what we call "Apostolic Succession" does not represent a narrow canonical principle, nor an external continuation, but rather indicates and signifies the presence of the Holy Spirit, that unique gift which holds the entire Church in continuity of the charismatic life.

3. WHEN adopting the view that Jesus Christ remains actively present, through the Holy Spirit, in the Christian priesthood, in fact we relate priesthood to the One God in Trinity, the Father, the Son and the Holy Spirit. In the Patristic understanding, both Christology and Pneumatology are always placed in their Trinitarian context.

Pseudo-Dionysius had in mind the Trinitarian dimension and perspective of priesthood, when he declared that the "source" of the ecclesiastical hierarchy "is the font of life, the being of goodness, the one cause of everything, namely, the Trinity which in goodness bestows being and well-being on everything".[6] The same notion is stressed by Saint Maximus the Confessor, who points out that "the true priesthood is in all respects the type of the blessed divinity".[7] Earlier, Saint Ignatius of Antioch recommended to the Trallians to "respect the deacons as Jesus Christ, even as they should respect the bishop as being a type of the Father and the presbyters as the council of God and as the college of Apostles".[8] In a spurious treatise, attributed to Saint Athanasius, a discussion is developed between an orthodox and an anomoean on the issue: "the bishop, the presbyter and the deacon, like the Father, the Son and the Holy Spirit".[9] A similar typology we find later, in the liturgical writings of Saint Symeon of Thessalonica. There, Christian priesthood is called "divine", a definition parallel to that of Saint Gregory of Nyssa, who described priesthood as "a divine matter" (*theion chrema*).[10] Saint Symeon following and quoting Pseudo-Dionysius says that "in the type of the Trinity we have these three: the deacon, the presbyter and the bishop".[11]

4. THE Trinitarian foundation of priestly order reveals and emphasizes not only the divine origin of the Christian priesthood, but equally its communal character. If the communion of the three divine persons, that of the Father and of the Son and of the Holy Spirit, is the communion *par excellence,* and if priesthood in its threefold aspect, bishop, presbyter, deacon, is an image and a type of the Holy Trinity, then, consequently, the priestly *diakonia* is an event of communion. Priesthood in its essence is a communal reality. It is a way of communion with God, that is, it is a peculiar communion in terms of the divine grace conferred in ordination. It is also an intercommunion of Church ministry and a *syndiakonia* between the three ranks of the ordained priesthood.

The priestly *diakonia*, as a sacramental consecration, is not an abstract and mysterious appointment but a concrete ministry deeply bound to the very being of the ecclesial communion. Through ordination every individual priest accepts a unique commission to serve a community. His mission is inseparably related and destined to a concrete ecclesial body. In the canonical tradition of the Eastern Church it is prohibited to ordain a person *in abstracto* and in a general sense. An ordination without a specific appointment is not acceptable. The ordained person should always be associated with a parish, with a concrete Christian community. The 6th canon of the Fourth Ecumenical Council, of Chalcedon, is absolutely clear: "No one should be ordained without a concrete appointment. Neither presbyter, nor deacon nor any other in the ecclesiastical rank. The ordained must be designated to serve in a concrete ecclesial community of a city or of a village or of a martyr's sanctuary or of a monastery. The Holy Council has ordered that an ordination without a concrctc appointment should be void and the person ordained should not have the right to serve anywhere. This punishment should be understood also as a disapproval of the bishop who ordained him."

The same is true of bishops. Assignment to a particular episcopal ministry is the *sine qua non* for his ordination. Bishop, priest and deacon alike should be assigned to a concrete diocese, or congregation. This spiritual relation is a kind of matrimonial connection. Thus, a cleric is appointed to serve the flock specifically assigned to him. In order to guarantee this unique communion between the ordained and his faithful the First Ecumenical Council in its 15th rule declared a direct prohibition for all clergy to move from one place to another. Neither a bishop, nor a priest, nor a deacon has the right to leave his place and go elsewhere.

Speaking of priesthood as a *diakonia* within the concrete ecclesial community, we should underline the communal character of the ordination service itself. In any circumstance secret ordination is absolutely unacceptable.[12] Ordination is always an ecclesial *praxis*; a spiritual action realized within the body of the Christian community; it is open and public, before the community and together with the community. It is not performed by the bishop or the bishops alone, but by the bishop or the bishops, together with the other clergy and the congregation. In eastern ordinations the "*Axios*", the "*Kyrie eleison*" and the "*Amen*", pronounced by the entire community, are not mere ceremonial exaltations, but a responsible testimony and a way of expressing ecclesial approval. This ecclesial approval is shown in a direct way by the exclamation pronounced by the deacon, both to the Bishop and to the congregation, before the ordination ceremony begins: "give the command" (*keleuson* in the singular, but also *keleusate* in the plural). These exaltations have deep ecclesiological significance.

This means that the ordination is performed by the bishop or the bishops together with the entire people of God. The bishop is not acting alone, but as the person who has the sacramental power to ordain within and together with the Christian community. He is the person charismatically appointed to safeguard the unity of the Church, connecting, by what we call Apostolic Succession, the present with the initial fulfilment.

The canonical tradition of Eastern Christendom and the patristic treatises are full of evidences and indications that all ordinations are inseparably connected with a given community, and through this concrete community with the catholic ecclesial body. Approaching the ordination of a bishop from this perspective, we can infer that the participation of at least three bishops has substantial ecclesiological meaning. The 4th rule of the First Ecumenical Council prescribes that the ordination of a bishop should be performed by all bishops of the district, and if this is not possible, because of practical difficulties, by at least three. Each bishop takes part in the ordination of the new one as the representative and living presence of his entire flock; and each bishop is a visible image of the Catholic Church. Thus, the new bishop who is appointed to serve in a concrete diocese, through his ordination, is related to the whole Church. The ordination of a bishop does not simply convey to the newly ordained juridical privileges, but elevates him to the relational rank of a catholic person, and places him in the midst of the community as a living image and testimony of the ecclesial oneness.

The same applies to the ordination of a priest. Through his ordination the new presbyter is again existentially related, in a unique and specific way, to the entire Body of the Church, thus becoming himself an instrument for the edification of ecclesial unity. This means that the ordination of a presbyter is not an isolated sacramental action, in itself and for itself, but a sacramental and spiritual event related to the concrete community, and through it to the life of the whole Church. If we maintain that the Risen Lord remains present in the eucharistic community through the power of the Holy Spirit, and if we profess, as we have already done, that the presbyter through his ordination is directly connected with the priesthood of Christ by that same Spirit, then we can assert that the ordained person, receiving the priesthood within the community and being a member of the Christian community, has the vocation and commission to serve, in cooperation with Christ and the community, for the establishment of the kingdom of God in the entire world. Thus, the *diakonia* of priesthood is not limited and exhausted to the given community, but in its eucharistic dimension is extended dynamically to the entire Christian body. Again, every priest becomes through his ordination and the offering of the eucharistic sacrifice a catholic person.

5. BOTH the bishop and the presbyter, as celebrants of the Holy Eucharist, are builders of the ecclesial unity. It is there, in the eucharistic bond, that all believers are united together in the one sacred relation to Christ, the living Lord. In the Eucharist the people of God are indeed in a constant, personal and at the same time communal relation to Christ, the risen Lord. It is no coincidence that all ordinations, already from earliest Christian times, are liturgically and theologically inseparable from the eucharistic communion. The fact that the eucharistic gathering is the unique and exclusive *locus* for all ministerial consecrations asserts that the priesthood belongs to the eucharistic community. It is begotten for the community, and because of this every consecration is realized within the context of the eucharistic assembly. It is the reality of the people of God, gathered together in the eucharistic communion, that constitutes the basis for the existence of the priestly *diakonia*. Priesthood was born for the Church and within the Church.

The implications of this perspective are of paramount importance for both a theology of priesthood and an understanding of its role for the ecclesial unity. The first point we should firmly stress once more is that priesthood cannot exist as such apart from the community. Priesthood is not an authority or a power above the community, neither a function nor an office parallel or outside it. Priesthood is indeed intrinsically related to the eucharistic sacrifice, which is the central empowering event and the source of unity of the ecclesial community. This means that the local community finds its unity in the priest, in the sense that through him it forms a eucharistic body, sacramentally linked and canonically conjoined with the catholic fullness of the Church. Through the *charisma* given to the ordained person, the ecclesial unity and catholicity is realized in a concrete place as eucharistic participation. Thus, priesthood exists as a *charisma* which belongs not to an individual but to a person who is dedicated to serve the community. The words of Christ, addressed to His disciples, are significant and clearly describe the otherness of the priestly service. "You know that the rulers of the Gentiles exercise dominion over them, and those who are great exercise authority over them. Yet it shall not be so among you; but whoever desires to become great among you, let him be your servant. And whoever desires to be first among you, let him be your slave – just as the Son of Man did not come to be served, but to serve, and give his life a ransom for many" (Matt. 20: 25–28; Mark 10: 42–45).

In his ordination the priest or bishop receives a power of a different level and order. One has to estimate this power in the light of the eucharistic gathering. In fact we cannot think of a gift "possessed individually",[13] neither of a juridical authority within the ecclesial body, but of a charismatic ministry belonging to all the people of God. One can talk of a divine economy, of a ministry which has catholic consequences and which ministers in the Eucharistic Synaxis as a force transforming the entire community to "a spiritual house, a holy priesthood, to offer up spiritual sacrifices acceptable to God through Jesus Christ" (1 Pet. 2: 5). Although priesthood elevates the community to the level of "a royal priesthood, a holy nation" (1 Pet. 2: 9), it is the community which has always been the permanent and the efficient basis of priesthood.

6. In the *Apology* of the monk Leontius of Jerusalem, which was appended to the Acts of the Fourth Ecumenical Council,[14] we find an unusual and interesting narration that illustrates our discussion. A mime actor of the theatre accused of subversive activity and homicide, fled his homeland in order to avoid arrest and judgement, retreating to the desert in a foreign land. After some time there, he once more met adversity, this time being taken hostage by certain Saracen Christians. These Christians, reckoning he was a priest because of his external appearance, demanded that he celebrate the Holy Eucharist for them. His attempts to persuade his captors otherwise were judged to be pious acts of humility prevalent among the holy ascetics. Not succeeding in convincing them, he gave in to their obstinate demands and agreed to perform the ritual. At his instructions, they built together an altar table out of wood and straw, setting over it a woven cloth and on this they placed the bread and wine in a wooden cup. The imprisoned actor sealed the gifts with the Sign and looking up to heaven, glorified the Holy Trinity. This was the only thing he did. After that he broke the bread and gave it to the Christians, taking the wooden vessel he gave them wine from the cup. Upon finishing the believers took with devotion the altar cloth and the cup, leaving behind only the altar. Just as they were leaving the place of worship, fire fell from heaven and burned the altar without touching or harming any of the faithful and yet consuming the altar entirely, leaving nothing remaining of it not even ashes. Beholding this awesome and frightening sign, the grateful Christians wanted to recompense the one whom they thought to be a priest, and asked him what he desired. He responded that the only thing he wanted was for him and those with him to be set free, and the Saracen Christians set them free.

7. LEONTIUS of Jerusalem, in his *Apology,* is not discussing Eucharistic theology. His intention was rather to expose the heresies of Nestorianism and Monophysiticim, and the possibility of miracles both in the Orthodox Church and in circles of schismatics and heretics. At any rate, the reference to Eucharist and priesthood, it seems to me, is useful for our discussion.

First of all, we observe that for the Christians in this narrative priesthood is understood as an undoubtedly necessary condition for their communal constitution. As a Christian group, as a small ecclesial community, they could not exist otherwise than in the

fellowship with him who has the gift and the power of sacramental action. It is through the priesthood that the Holy Spirit
abides in their fraternal gathering, transfiguring it to a pentecostal
body. Although the person chosen to celebrate the Eucharist was
not in fact ordained, the Saracen Christians took it for granted
that he was a priest. There was not any doubt among them that
their community is fulfilled and integrated through the priestly
ministry. Their communal being was precisely transformed into
an ecclesial being through and in priesthood.

The second point we ought to stress is that for the people
in the narrative of Leontius, the Eucharist was considered as an
indispensable necessity for their spiritual being, as a sacrament
decisive for their ecclesial existence. Obviously, Eucharist here is
not seen as an objectified ritual, disassociated from their corporate
identity, but flows from the community itself. Indeed, Eucharist
needs to be apprehended as a gift related to the community, both
to the minister and the "*laos*". Nicholas Cabasilas says that the
Eucharist is a command of Christ "to the Apostles and through
the Apostles to the whole Church".[15] In this sense, the Eucharist
is not the *praxis* of an ordained individual, but that of a community,
that is, performed by the priest together with the people. The
Eucharist is a liturgical *praxis*; liturgical in the etymological sense
of the term, "work of the people" (*ergon laou*), not of one single
minister isolated from the ecclesial community. In the final
analysis the protagonist in the Eucharist is Christ Himself Who,
through the priest and the community, builds up His Body.

8. THIS approach leads us to the understanding that the priest
does not possess in himself an "indelible mark", as if it were a
magical seal which grants him a private efficacy to perform the
Eucharist or any other liturgical action, apart from the ecclesial
body. The priestly ministry is rather a charismatic gift for the
purpose of serving and edifying the Body of the Church. It is a
permanent rank of service only in union and by the discerning
authority of the Church.

The doctrine of the "indelible mark" attained at ordination
to the priesthood appears to have originated in the Scholastic

period of the Western Church. This same conception was at times borrowed by Eastern theologians thereafter. The teaching purports the grace of ordination as an indelible irrevocable mark upon the soul of the ordained individual that sets him apart for priestly service analogous to the Levite rank and the priesthood according to the order of Melchizedek in the Old Testament. It is interesting to mention here that the 6th Ecumenical Council in its 33rd canon condemns the practice of Armenian Christians who had embraced the Old Testament custom concerning the Levitic rank and did not accept for the priesthood anyone who was not of this so-called "priestly lineage". The reasoning for the adoption of the Old Testament typology, in both cases, seems to be that an identification mark is a constitutive element of priesthood. In the latter case it is conceived as an inherited trait, while in the former, which concerns us here, it is viewed as irrevocably and individually attained at the ordination rite.

The logical conclusion of the "indelible mark" is that the ordained individual possesses forever this peculiar mark of priesthood which can never be removed by anyone, nor can it be surrendered in any circumstance. It is evident that such a doctrinal consideration absolutizes and isolates priesthood from the very event of ecclesial communion. Priesthood here is distortingly objectified and over-estimated, assuming a totalitarian magnitude. It is imposed on the Church, which is unable to deprive the ordained individual of its characteristic mark, even if he is unworthy to maintain the ecclesial grace. In fact the doctrine of the "indelible mark" divorces the priesthood from its organic context of the ecclesial life. Thus the ordained person possesses a self-sufficient power, higher than the Church itself. And the Church is not able to take back the indelible mark from an individual even if he is defrocked and excommunicated.

Interpreting the 68th Apostolic Canon, which refers to the impossibility of repeating the sacrament of ordination,[16] Saint Nicodimos the Hagiorite explains that ordination cannot be repeated because it is done according to the Type of the First and Great Priest who entered once and for all into the Holy of

Holies and there granted eternal salvation. Yet, he unswervingly rejects the doctrine of the "indelible mark" of priesthood, and protests that it is the "invention of scholastics".[17] Nevertheless, according to Saint Nicodimos, the doctrine is borrowed by Nicholas Bulgaris, Koresios and many other theologians of the past century, and some still somehow adhere to it today.

Despite the fact that the "indelible mark" theory acquired dogmatic formulation in the Council of Trent,[18] in most circles of the Roman Catholic Church, after the Second Vatican Council, the foundational framework of efficient causality and *ex opere operato,* which gave rise to such an understanding of priesthood, is regarded as belonging to a bygone age and abandoned for a more dynamic and ecclesiological approach of sacrament.[19]

It should be mentioned in this connection that, as far as we know, no evidence concerning the theory of the "indelible mark" can be found in Patristic teaching. On the contrary, the canonical data leave no doubt that a defrocked priest or bishop, after the decision of the Church to take back his priesthood, returns to the rank of the laity. The anathematized or the defrocked are in no way considered as retaining their priesthood. The canonical tradition that in the case of ministerial rehabilitation a person is not re-ordained does not imply a recognition that he was a priest during the period of his punishment.[20] It simply means that the Church recognizes that which had been sacramentally performed, and that the grace of ecclesiastical ministry is restored upon his assignment to an ecclesial community with no other sacramental sign or rite.

9. IN the light of what has been said thus far, we may conclude by saying that priesthood is in no way a ministry introducing division or classification within the ecclesial body. Between a priest and a lay person there is no legal distinction, but precisely what we may call charismatic distribution. As we read in First Corinthians 12:4–6, "There are diversities of gifts, but the same Spirit. There are differences of ministry but the same Lord. And there are diversities of activities, but it is the same God who works all in all." This means that through ordination a member of the Church is set apart in order to minister the sacrament of ecclesial unity. In the Patristic tradition, priesthood is never understood as an office based on an objectified mark imprinted on the soul of the ordained person, but rather as an ecclesial gift, as a vocation aiming to edify the Body of Christ. It has been rightly said that an Orthodox understanding of priesthood is beyond any "ontological" or "functional" definition.[21] Priesthood cannot be considered in itself and for itself, but rather as relational reality. In other words, the only way to have an adequate understanding of the priestly *charisma* is to see it in its *anaphoral* dimension and in connection with ecclesial communion.

NOTES

* Paper delivered as the keynote address for the Twelfth International Congress of the Society for the Law of the Eastern Churches, Boston MA, 20–26 August 1995, first published in *Kanon* 13 (1996), 135–147.

1. J. Zizioulas, *L'être ecclésial* (Paris, 1981), p. 171.

2. *Cf.* Ignatius of Antioch, *To the Smyrnaeans* 9: " . . . *Christon Iesoun, ton prototokon kai monon te physei tou Patros archierea*".

3. *Cf.* Justin Martyr, *Dialogue* 42, 1: " . . . *apo tes dynameos tou aioniou hiereos Christou*".

4. N. Nissiotis, "The Importance of the Doctrine of the Trinity for Church Life and Theology", in *The Orthodox Ethos* (Oxford, 1964), p. 39.

5. G. Florovsky, "The Sacrament of Pentecost", in *Creation and Redemption* (Belmont MA, 1976), p. 190.

6. Pseudo-Dionysius, *The Ecclesiastical Hierarchy* (PG 3:373C).

7. Maximus the Confessor, *Letter to Bishop John* (PG 91:625A): " . . . *he alethes hierosyne charakter esti dia panton tes makarias theotetos*".

8. Ignatius of Antioch, *To the Trallians* 3, 1. See also *To the Magnesians* 6, 1.

9. Athanasius of Alexandria, *Dialogue on the Holy Trinity* 27 (PG 28:1156 ff).

10. Gregory of Nyssa, *Life of Moses* II, 130, 15–16, ed. H. Musurillo (Leiden and New York, 1991); PG 44:417B.

11. Symeon of Thessalonica, *On Holy Ordinations* (PG 155:364A).

12. Florovsky, *op. cit.*, p. 192.

13. Zizioulas, *op. cit.*, p. 164.

14. J. D. Mansi, *Sacrorum Conciliorum Nova et Amplissima Collectio*, Vol. 7 (Graz, 1960, repr. ed.), 8, 821–824.

15. Nicholas Cabasilas, *A Commentary on the Divine Liturgy* 28.

16. See also Canon 48 of the Council of Carthage.

17. "*Hoi scholastikoi legoun dioti aphinoun kai typonoun auta charaktera anexaleipton, hos tis kat' auntous poiotes pragmatike enhyparchousa te psyche kai dynameis hyperphyes*", *The Pedalion* (Athens, 1970), p. 90. "*Ho para ton scholastikon epinoetheis charakter . . .*", *ibid.*

18. Canon 4: "*Si quis dixerit, per sacram ordinationem non dari Spiritum sanctum, ac proinde frustra episcopos dicere: Accipe Spiritum Sanctum; aut per eam non imprimi characterem; vel eum, qui sacerdos semel fuit, laicum rursus fieri posse, anathema sit.*"

19. See for example, B. Cooke, *Ministry to Word and Sacraments: History and Theology* (Philadelphia PA, 1978, 3rd repr. ed.), 187 ff. T. O'Meara, "Orders and Ordination", in *The New Dictionary of Theology* (Collegeville MN, 1991), 725–726.

20. Zizioulas, *op. cit.*, p. 233.

21. *Ibid.*, pp. 226–227.

"Never as Gods"
Icons and their Veneration*

I N THE TRADITION OF THE EASTERN CHURCH
doctrine and worship are inseparable. Worship is, in a
certain sense, doctrinal testimony, reference to the events
of Revelation. Thus "dogmas are not abstract ideas in and for
themselves but revealed and saving truths and realities intended
to bring mankind into communion with God".[1] One could say
without hesitation that, according to Orthodox understanding,
the fullness of theological thought is found in the worship of the
Church. This is why the term Orthodoxy is understood by many
not as "right opinion", but as "right doxology", "right worship".
Right worship is bound up with right opinion.

In this perspective of the close relationship between
worship and doctrine, I am of the opinion that the best way
to present a brief theology of icons is to use liturgical data.
That is, to consider the doctrinal testimony of the worshipping community. Thus I will take as a basis for my paper three
hymns from the Sunday of Orthodoxy. As is well known, the
Sunday of Orthodoxy is the first Sunday in Lent, when the
Orthodox Church commemorates her victory over the iconoclasts and the final restoration of icons to the churches by

the empress Theodora, regent of her young son Michael III. This restoration took place at a synod held at Constantinople in 843, which decreed that in commemoration of this event a Feast of Orthodoxy should be celebrated annually. The three hymns I shall use as a frame of reference for my paper are: the *kontakion*; the third *sticheron*; and the *doxasticon* of Vespers.[2]

The uncircumscribed Word of the Father became circumscribed, taking flesh from thee, O Theotokos, and He has restored the sullied image to its ancient glory, filling it with the divine beauty. This our salvation we confess in deed and word, and we depict it in the holy icons.

Thou who art uncircumscribed, O Master, in Thy divine nature, wast pleased in the last times to take flesh and be circumscribed; and in assuming flesh, Thou hast also taken on Thyself all its distinctive properties. Therefore we depict the likeness of Thine outward form, venerating it with an honour that is relative. So we are exalted to the love of Thee, and following the holy traditions handed down by the apostles, from Thine icon we receive the grace of healing.

Advancing from ungodliness to the true faith, and illumined with the light of knowledge, let us clap our hands and sing aloud, offering praise and thanksgiving to God; and with due honour let us venerate the holy icons of Christ, of the all-pure Virgin and the saints, whether depicted on walls, on wooden panels or on holy vessels, rejecting the impious teaching of the heretics. For, as Basil says, the honour shown to the icon passes to the prototype it represents. At the prayers of Thine undefiled Mother and of all the saints, we beseech Thee, Christ our God, to bestow upon us Thy great mercy.

"The uncircumscribed Word of the Father, taking flesh, became circumscribed"

STUDYING the issue of icons we can easily realize that the whole matter has a christological dimension. The use of icons forms an integral part of the doctrine of the Incarnation. The main question could be formulated as follows: Was Christ, the incarnate Logos of the Father, circumscribed or uncircumscribed? The iconoclasts declared that Christ was uncircumscribed, as God-Man, for the unity of divinity and humanity allowed no room for depicting him. According to the theology of the iconoclasts, as presented at the Council of Hieria (754),[3] the iconographer painting an icon of Christ represents either his humanity, separating it from the divinity, or both the humanity and the divinity of the incarnate Logos. In the first instance he is a follower of Nestorius, while in the second he confuses divinity and humanity, and follows the Monophysites; even worse, he assumes that the uncircumscribed divine nature can be circumscribed by humanity, which is of course blasphemous.[4]

Although these arguments appear reasonable, it is evident that the iconoclasts had difficulties understanding that an icon does not represent either the one or the two natures of Christ. An icon is rather a representation of the invisible through the visible. Saint John of Damascus, answering the objections of iconoclasts, makes the following clear theological statement:

> I do not venerate the creation over the Creator, but I venerate the Creator who became creation like me, and came down into creation without humiliation and without being debased, in order to glorify my nature and make me to be a partaker of the divine nature . . . For the nature of flesh has not become deity, but, as the Word became flesh without change, remaining as he was, likewise the flesh became Word, without losing what it is, identifying moreover with the Word hypostatically. Thus, taking courage, I represent God, the invisible, not as invisible, but insofar as he has become visible for us by participation in flesh and blood. I do not represent the invisible deity but I represent the flesh of God which has been seen.[5]

Besides the arguments brought against the use of icons one can see a deep theological difference between iconoclasts and defenders of the icons. Emphasis was given to the nature by the iconoclasts, while for the supporters of the icons the hypostasis, the person of the incarnated Word served as the foundation. Saint Theodore the Studite gives us the orthodox position briefly and clearly: "Every image is the image of an hypostasis, and never of a nature."[6] Seen from this perspective, an icon is an historical picture. Thus the maker of an icon does not depict images of certain invisible, heavenly and transcendental realities, but concrete events and personalities connected with the historic fact of the Incarnation.

The icon is understood as a gift of the Incarnation, as a new possibility to theologize, based on the person of the Son incarnate.

In Old Testament times there could not be any possibility of representing God. In the Mosaic law there is a strict prohibition concerning images: "Thou shalt not make unto thee any graven image, or any likeness of any thing" (Exod. 20:4).[7] Images constituted at that time a danger to the worship of the one and true God. Again Saint John of Damascus declares:

> In times past, God, without body and form, could in no way be represented. But now, since God has appeared in flesh and lived among men, I can depict that which is visible of God. I do not venerate the matter, but I venerate the Creator of matter, who became matter for me, who condescended to live in matter, and who, through matter accomplished my salvation; and I do not cease to respect the matter through which my salvation is accomplished.[8]

In Christ, matter is assumed and sanctified. The mystery of the divine economy constitutes the definite abolition of any dualism between spirit and matter. In the person of Christ we find the affirmation of matter, which becomes the medium of divine energy and grace.[9] Thus matter has a certain liturgical function in the history of salvation.

So it is from this perspective that we ought to understand the accusation of idolatry put forward by the iconoclasts. In Greek pagan religion, idols were pictures of things which did not exist in reality.[10] In such cases, matter does become an object of worship (*adoratio*). In the New Testament, however, Christ delivers men from idolatry not in a negative way, by abolishing any image, but positively, by revealing himself, who is the true image of God the Father (2 Cor. 4:4; Col. 1:15; *cf.* John 14:9).[11] In his divinity the Word of God is the consubstantial image of the Father, and in his humanity he is the image of God. In his humanity he reveals the image of the authentic man. This is self-evident even though we can not separate the two natures in Christ. (Such a division would lead either to Nestorianism or to Monophysitism.) The reality of the hypostasis, of the one Person of Christ, ensures the unity of the two natures "without confusion, without change, without division, without separation".[12] And thus when speaking of Christ we presuppose the unity of the two natures.

In an analogous way, when speaking of the icon of Christ we take for granted this unity in the icon; in other words we do not have in the icon the image of the humanity of Christ, separated from his divinity, but rather we understand that this image is a representation of the one incarnated Logos, of the uncircumscribed Word of the Father, who, taking flesh, became circumscribed. As the hypostasis assures the unity as well as the distinction of the two natures, the icon of Christ likewise testifies to this unity of the natures and to the distinction between created and uncreated.[13]

In order to justify the possibility of painting an image of Christ, the Fathers of the Seventh Ecumenical Council clearly underlined this appearance of the icon of the very hypostasis of God the Logos in the flesh:

> The Catholic Church while depicting Christ in his human form, does not separate it from the divinity united unto it; rather she considers it as being deified and confesses it as wholly one with God [*omotheon*], as Gregory the Theologian also states . . . And just as when one paints the picture of a man he does not depict him without his soul, but rather he who is depicted remains with his soul . . . so, too, when making the icon of the Lord, we confess his flesh to be deified and we understand his icon as nothing else but an icon showing the imitation of the prototype.[14]

"He has restored the sullied image to its ancient glory, filling it with the divine beauty"

ICONS have their biblical justification in the creation of man according to the divine image. The creation of man "in the image of God", "after his likeness" (Gen. 1:26–27), clearly demonstrates that there is a certain analogy between the divine and the human. The Greek Fathers understood this analogy in terms of participation in the divine beauty. From this perspective, the fact that man was created in the image of God means that God made human nature a participant of every good. By virtue of his own nature God himself is the absolute beauty and good. And thus in creating man according to his image he has communicated to him his own goodness, which is described as freedom, wisdom, justice, love, immortality.[15] In other words, man was created to be a kind of mirror reflecting the divine beauty. It is self-evident that there is a basic difference between God the prototype and man the image: the latter is created, while the former is uncreated. It is remarkable also that the creation of man according to the divine image was a dynamic vocation. Man should extend himself from the image to the likeness of God. The gift of the image did not have a static character; it was rather the beginning of a personal history of sanctification. But the image of God as created reality was still characterized by changeability. Man could refuse to follow the way leading from image to likeness. In fact this is precisely what happened: by his free will he fell. Original sin is understood as the darkening and obscuring of the divine image. Saint Gregory of Nyssa says that man has changed the image for a mask (*prosopeion*).[16]

It was by the Incarnation of the Logos that man was restored to his ancient glory. In Christ is realized a second creation of man; the hidden and obscured image of God was repainted. The way from the image to the likeness is again open for man. The fact that the Son of God became man gives man the possibility of becoming himself god by grace. The Fathers of the Seventh Ecumenical Council, comparing the first creation to the second, point out that the second creation of man, realized by God the Logos, "is more in God's likeness and thus the recreation becomes a better thing than the creation; and this gift is eternal".[17]

This "inalienable gift"[18] brings man once more into communion with the divine beauty. Again man is given the possibility to become, freely and consciously, a God-bearer (*theophoros*). Certainly the *locus* of this transfiguration of man is the Church. Through baptism in the Church man can find his real being. In other words, the Church offers a cure and a healing, returning man to his natural state. And so man in the Church, participating in the life of the deity, himself becomes an icon. Saint Diadochus of Photice points out that man in the Church, through inner action and the grace of the Holy Spirit, is given the possibility "to repaint his own likeness on the image of God".[19]

This iconic dimension of man is clearly indicated in many aspects of the life of the Orthodox Church. In every Liturgy and public act of worship the priest offers incense to every one of the faithful in the same way as he offers it to the icons. In the divine Liturgy, the believers who sing the thrice-holy hymn to the life-giving Trinity are considered to be images of the cherubim. Surrounded by the icons, they offer to Christ his own from his own, in all and for all. And so the Liturgy is a living icon of the heavenly mystery of the kingdom of God. Even the Church building, says Saint Symeon of Thessalonica, is an image of the Church in her totality, representing what is on earth, what is in the heavens, and what is beyond the heavens. The narthex of the Church corresponds to the earth, the nave to paradise or the heavens, the sanctuary to that which is higher than the heavens.[20] Moreover, the Church itself is an icon of the Holy Trinity. The communion of persons in the body of the Church is in the image of the communion of the divine Persons.

In the light of what has been said it is easy to understand that the use of icons has a deep theological significance. We would do better to say that icons are in themselves theology, "word about God", intended to bring man to the "face to face" vision of God, which transcends words, concepts and images. The painting of icons involves a visual representation of the entire drama of human history. The creation of man in the image of God, his recreation in Christ, his transfiguration and his final glory, are all, in a certain sense, present in "the holy icons of Christ, of the all-pure Virgin and the saints, whether depicted on the walls, on wooden panels or on holy vessels".

"We confess our salvation in deed and word, and we depict it in the holy icons"

SAINT John Damascene, in his *On the Divine Images* I, reminds us of the distinction made by Saint Basil the Great between written and unwritten doctrine, and he underlines his conclusion that "both have equal force for piety".[21] He follows the same line himself when he speaks of the "unwritten customs", emphasizing that "the ecclesiastical ordinance is transmitted to us not only through letters but also through unwritten traditions".[22]

We have to see the role of icons in the life of the Church within this context. We have already said that through the Incarnation of the Word of God man becomes a new creation, becoming himself an icon by the grace of the Holy Spirit and by inner action. We have also suggested that icons are another way of theologizing. In the final analysis, this means that in the Church man receives two possibilities: firstly, to become the image of God, thereby restoring God's likeness in himself; and secondly, to proclaim this gift to his fellow man, theologizing to this end not only in verbal, but also in visual images.[23]

Icons are words in painting; they refer to the history of salvation and to its manifestation in concrete persons. In the Orthodox Church icons have always been understood as a visible gospel, as a testimony to the great things given man by God the incarnate Logos. In the Council of 860 it was stated that "all that is uttered in words written in syllables is also proclaimed in the language of colours".[24] From this perspective icons and Scripture are linked through an inner relationship; both coexist in the Church and proclaim the same truths. There is a mutual supplementation and agreement between words and visual images. Scripture, says Saint John of Damascus, is a kind of icon. And the icon, from another point of view, is Holy Scripture. I return once more to his formulation:

Just as in the Bible we listen to the word of Christ and are sanctified . . . in the same way through the painted icons we behold the representation of his human form, of his miracles and passion, and are likewise sanctified, and fully reassured, and imbued with joy, and pronounced blessed; and we respect, honour and venerate his human form. And beholding his human form, we contemplate, as much as we can, the glory of his deity. Because we can only arrive at the spiritual through the material, for we are created twofold, possessing both soul and body; and because our soul is not naked but covered with a veil, thus we hear comprehensible words as with our corporeal ears and consequently contemplate the spiritual; and thus through bodily vision we come to the spiritual.[25]

The iconic dimension of Scripture and the scriptural dimension of icons correspond absolutely to the theology of the Eastern Church, and especially to its teaching concerning revelation and the knowledge of God. It is well known that from an Orthodox viewpoint the words of the Bible are not revelation in themselves, but rather words concerning revelation.[26] In the same way, an icon is not itself independent, but rather guides us to that which is. From this perspective both Scripture and icons have an introductory and a pedagogic function. Both mediate historical events or historical persons. In both is salvation confessed; in the first through words, in the second through depiction. Both indicate the revelation, although revelation itself transcends words and images alike.[27] It is remarkable that Nicephorus, Patriarch of Constantinople (806–815), considered that icons, although a more "earthly scripture", have a powerful influence, especially on those who do not understand Scripture. Indeed, very often what escapes us when hearing words does not escape us when viewing icons.[28] For their part the Fathers of the Seventh Ecumenical Council speak about the "scriptural vision" and the "pictorial formation" as the two symbolic ways through which we reach the supra-sensible realities.[29]

Nevertheless, the introductory and instructive character of both Holy Scripture and icons needs further clarification. Speaking of Scripture and icons as symbolic ways (symbolic in the primitive meaning of this Greek word), we simply mean that both have a limited function, since the mystery of God itself and the experience, the glory of the transfigured Christ and the unspeakable words heard by Saint Paul, are revealed realities, which cannot be expressed and transmitted in created words, concepts or images. Saint Symeon the New Theologian refers to 2 Corinthians 12:3–4 ["And I knew such a man, (whether in the body, or out of the body, I cannot tell: God knoweth;) How that he was caught up into paradise, and heard unspeakable words, which it is not lawful for a man to utter"], and comments:

The "unspeakable words" are the mystical and truly inexpressible visions and supra-exalted unknown knowledge of the glory and deity of the Son and Word of God which is beyond light and which transcends knowledge. This revelation of the glory of God [called by Symeon the apprehension, in incomprehensibility, of things that cannot be grasped] is given to the saints by the illumination of the Holy Spirit.[30]

Thus the saints, through divine illumination, come to hear the unspeakable words, which are above any hearing; they have a vision of what is above every vision. According to Saint Symeon, the man who has achieved illumination and has come to the vision of God has a new sense which is the unification of all the five senses and at the same time is above every sense.[31] With this in mind it is possible to understand that scriptural, as well as pictorial, knowledge concerning God leads to a supra-intellectual and supra-sensible knowledge of God. Such knowledge is contained in the Bible and expressed by means of icons (since every icon manifests that which is hidden);[32] and yet it is above any description of, or any expression concerning, God, either in Holy Scripture or the icons.

"We depict the likeness of thine outward form, venerating it with an honour that is relative"

AT this point we must touch on the very delicate question of the veneration of icons. This was one of the basic issues between those involved in the long iconoclastic controversy; it was also the cause of many misunderstandings in Western Christianity. A characteristic example of this is the twenty-second of the Anglican "Articles of Religion", where "the worship and adoration of images" is condemned. Since these misunderstandings are, to a large degree, the result of difficulties in translation, it may be worthwhile to make a brief clarification of the terms used. Basically, two words are used in Greek: *aspasmos* and *proskynêsis*. We can translate the first as "greeting" and the second as "veneration". Both terms are included in the definition of the Seventh Ecumenical Council, and even veneration is defined as a "veneration of honour" (*timêtikê proskynêsis*):

We decree with all precision and care that the venerable and holy icons are to be set up alongside the form of the venerable and life-giving cross; these consisting of colours and mosaics and other suitable material, are to be set up in the holy churches of God, on sacred vessels and vestments, on walls and panels, in houses and by the wayside: both the image of our Lord, God and Saviour Jesus Christ, and of our spotless Lady the holy Mother of God, of the honourable angels and of all holy and pious men. For the more frequently they are seen

by means of pictorial representation the more are those who behold
them aroused to remember and desire their prototypes and to give
them greeting and the veneration of honour: not indeed that true
worship [*latreia*] which, according to our faith, is due to God alone.[33]

Although the definition of the Council is very clear and excludes
any kind of *latreia*, the actual worship of icons was often attributed to
Eastern Christianity. Obviously this is due to the unfortunate translation of the Greek *proskynêsis,* "veneration", as *adoratio* in the Latin
version of the Conciliar Acts. The famous *Libri Carolini* used this translation and rejected, for political reasons, both the Iconoclastic Council
of 754 and Nicaea II of 787. Nicaea II was characterized in the Caroline
Books as *ineptissimae Synodi*. It is remarkable that Thomas Aquinas,
who accepted Nicaea II, was to speak of a "relative adoration". Basing
their arguments on this expression the Greeks took the opportunity to
accuse the Latins of idolatry in a Council held at Sancta Sophia in 1450.[34]

At any rate, and in spite of misinterpretations, Orthodox
theology has always clearly stated that the veneration of
icons has a relative character. The Fathers of the Seventh
Ecumenical Council often repeat: "Christians respect one God
praised in Trinity, and him alone do they worship." And thus, in
approaching the icons, "they venerate them relatively . . . and
indeed never as gods".[35]

"The honour shown to the icon passes to the prototype it represents"

THE Platonic conception of the "prototype" and the "image"
was used a great deal in the iconoclastic controversy. To the
iconoclastic identification of the image with the prototype the
defenders of the icons proposed the real distinction of the icon
from the divine model. Icons remind us of the prototypes and
elevate us to them.[36] They are not realities in themselves, but
their value derives from the realities they represent. Icons are
signs of the invisible presence of God in history. They guide us
to a vision of a new history, the vision of the divine kingdom in
which past, present and future are contained. They are entrances
into another cosmos, which is to be revealed in its fullness at
the end of time. The analogy "image–prototype" requires some

further elaboration. We take as a basis the classical formulation derived from Saint Basil the Great: "The honour shown to the icon passes to the prototype it represents."[37]

Speaking here of the icon and the prototype we do not mean a relationship analogous to that of the divine persons. Only the Son is "the natural and in no way differing image" of the Father, and only the Spirit "the natural and in no way differing image" of the Son.[38] Other images of God are different from their model, and therefore not idols.[39] Although an icon is distinct from its prototype, yet there is a close relationship between them. In other words, the icons of the saints are not just pictures of some models of the past, but witnesses in the here and now of the life of holiness. The deacon Stephanus of Constantinople in his *Vita Sancti Stephani Junioris* points out that "the icon is a door opening our mind, which is created after God, to the inner likeness of the prototype".[40] And Saint John Damascene, speaking of the icons, emphasizes that during their lives "the saints were filled with the Holy Spirit, and when they reposed the grace of the Holy Spirit remained in their souls and bodies, in their tombs, their engravings and their holy icons: indeed not by nature, but by grace and energy".[41] Thus the icon of a saint signifies his holiness. Consequently, when we honour it we do not honour a wooden panel or a wall or a vessel, but the sanctity of a concrete person. And yet, in honouring a saint we glorify and honour God from whom comes down every good and perfect gift. There is always a theological analogy, a Christocentric relation. "We depict the icon of Christ as King and Lord, never separating him from his army. The saints are the army of Christ . . . I venerate the icon of Christ as God incarnate; [the icon] of . . . the *Theotokos*, as Mother of the Son of God; [the icons] of the saints, as friends of God."[42]

The honour shown to icons refers back to our prototype, to the incarnate Son of God and, through him and in him, to the consubstantial and undivided Trinity. The words of Germanus, Patriarch of Constantinople, are significant in this connection: "When someone who is knowledgeable looks at the icon of a saint he says . . . Glory be to God, and he adds the name of the saint . . . that the all-holy name of Christ may be glorified in both the visible and invisible."[43]

"Following the holy traditions . . . from thine icon we receive the grace of healing"

IT is evident that when we speak of icons we touch on a very basic theme of Orthodox spirituality. Saint Germanus of Constantinople, speaking of the icons, takes up the words of John Chrysostom again, when he insists that the whole question of icons is filled with devotion.[44] In the Orthodox tradition it is commonly agreed that the icon is a living *memorandum* of the divine energy,[45] and even more a *medium* for receiving healing and grace. We have already pointed out that the sanctity of the saints is not simply a phenomenon of the past, but by grace is ever present in the icon "without departure". Thus the icons are sanctifying channels, ways of spiritual and bodily therapy and preludes to the final transfiguration of the world.

In order to understand the healing and charismatic dimensions of icons we should keep in mind what has already been briefly pointed out concerning matter. Since man is created of soul and body, it is only through the material that he can reach the spiritual. Thus matter has a liturgical function; it is something *sine qua non* not only in the earthly presence of Christ, which involved a continuous sanctification of matter, but also in the entire life of the Church. "I do not cease to respect matter through which my salvation is accomplished", notes Saint John Damascene, "because it is filled with divine energy and grace."[44] In the divine theophany, matter was assumed and used; it was restored and honoured. The wooden cross, the mountain, the place of the skull, the life-giving stone, the new tomb (the source of our resurrection), the Bible, the Holy Table where we partake of the Bread of Life, even the Body and the Blood of Christ themselves, are all matter.[47] Like these, and many other things, the icon is a material object through which grace is conveyed.

The granting of the grace of healing through material objects is a common tradition in the Church, and has its biblical foundation in the various miraculous healings performed by Christ and the apostles. We can recall, for example, the case of the woman who had an issue of blood twelve years, and who, just by touching the garment of Christ, was healed (Mark 5:25–34). Patriarch Germanus also reminds us of several stories from the Acts of the Apostles: the shadow of Peter (Acts 5:15–16), the handkerchiefs and the aprons of Paul (Acts 19:11–12) were also media of healing. Not every shadow or every handkerchief, but the shadow of Peter and the handkerchiefs of Paul. In an analogous way, not every icon is miraculous, only some of them. For the grace of healing is not automatically provided; it is given to the faithful under certain conditions as a gift of divine grace.[48]

Thus it is evident that the icon is not an element of decoration, but a liturgical object. This means that the icon is inseparable from the worshipping community, which elevates it to a means of receiving sanctifying and healing grace. For the basis of the grace of healing is the Church. Within the Church, the icon becomes a way for spiritual and bodily therapy, just as the Bible in the Church becomes a word of God "quick, and powerful, and sharper than any two-edged sword". Outside the Church, the icon is simply a religious picture, just as the Bible is a book "sealed with seven seals".

As the Gospel constitutes a surpassing of the standards of this world, so also the icon. The Gospel involves the abolition of human wisdom. The preaching of the cross is foolishness for the world (1 Cor. 1: 18). And yet, this foolishness is the destruction of all wisdom "after the flesh" (1 Cor. 1:26):

I will destroy the wisdom of the wise, and will bring to nothing the understanding of the prudent. Where is the wise? where is the scribe? where is the disputer of this world? hath not God made foolish the wisdom of this world? For after that in the wisdom of God the world by wisdom knew not God, it pleased God by the foolishness of preaching to save them that believe (1 Cor. 1:19–21).

Like the oral Gospel, the icon – this visual Gospel – is foolishness and scandal for the world. For the world is used to seeing things as they appear. Whereas the icon is a window which allows us to see things as they truly are, glorified and transfigured.[49]

NOTES

* A paper given at the Anglican–Orthodox Joint Doctrinal Commission held at Odessa in September, 1983, and first published in *Sobornost* 6 (1984), 6–18.

1. "Agreed Statement of the Third Sub-Commission (July 1982)", *Anglican–Orthodox Joint Doctrinal Discussions*, Document 257.

2. I borrow the English translation from *The Lenten Triodion*, trans. Mother Mary and Archimandrite Kallistos Ware (London, 1978), pp. 306, 300, 301, respectively.

3. The Acts of the Council of Hieria are preserved in the minutes of the Seventh Ecumenical Council (787).

4. For a brief exposition of Iconoclastic theology, see J. Meyendorff, *Byzantine Theology: Historical Trends and Doctrinal Themes* (New York, 1974), p. 44. See also G. Florovsky, "The Iconoclastic Controversy", *Christianity and Culture* (Belmont MA, 1974), pp. 101–119; and B. Giannopoulos, *Ai Christologikai antilepseis ton Ikonomachon* [The Christological Presuppositions of the Iconoclasts] (Athens, 1975).

5. PG 94:1236BC.

6. PG 99:405A.

7. On this point see the discussion in Saint John Damascene, PG 94:1245A ff and 1249D ff.

8. PG 94:1245AB.

9. PG 94:1300B.

10. Germanus of Constantinople, PG 98:152C.

11. See P. Evdokimov, *L'Orthodoxie* (Neuchâtel, 1965), p. 218.

12. *Definition of Faith*, Fourth Ecumenical Council (451).

13. Evdokimov, *L'art de l'icône. Théologie de beauté* (Paris, 1972), p. 178.

14. J. D. Mansi, *Sacrorum Conciliorum Nova et Amplissima Collectio*, Vol. xiii, 344AB.

15. See Gregory of Nyssa, PG 44:184AD. On the subject of participation in God's perfections according to Saint Gregory of Nyssa, see D. L. Balas, *Metousia Theou* (Rome, 1966), esp. p. 143. On the theme of man as the

image of God in connection with icons, see L. Ouspensky, *Théologie de l'icône* (Paris, 1980), p. 137 ff.

16. PG 44:193C.

17. Mansi, *op. cit.*, xiii, 216A.

18. *Ibid.*

19. *Philokalia* i (Athens, 1957), p. 266.

20. PG 155:292A, 337D–340A.

21. PG 94:1256A; and *cf.* Saint Basil: PG 32:188A ff.

22. *Ibid.*

23. See Ouspensky, in L. Ouspensky and V. Lossky, *The Meaning of Icons* (Boston MA, 1952), p. 37.

24. Mansi, *op. cit.*, xvi. 40D. See also Evdokimov, *L'Orthodoxie, op. cit.*, p. 222.

25. PG 94:1333D-1336B.

26. On this question, see Symeon the New Theologian, *Sources Chrétiennes* 122 (Paris, 1966), pp. 390–440. Saint Symeon's main point is that the Bible cannot be identified with revelation; he provides an excellent commentary on the unwritten words heard by Saint Paul.

27. "Just like the Holy Scripture, the icon transmits historical fact, an event from Sacred History or an historical personage, depicted in his real physical form and, again like the Holy Scripture, it indicates the revelation that is outside time, contained in a given historical reality" (Ouspensky, *The Meaning of Icons, op. cit.*, p. 37).

28. PG 100:380D.

29. Mansi, *op. cit.*, xiii, 482DE.

30. *Sources Chrétiennes* 122, pp. 398–400.

31. *Ibid.*, pp. 400–402.

32. John Damascene, PG 94:1337B.

33. Mansi, *op. cit.*, xiii, 377CDE.

34. Meyendorff, *Byzantine Theology, op. cit.*, p. 46.

35. Mansi, *op. cit.*, xiii, 482BC.

36. *Ibid.*, 482E.

37. *On the Holy Spirit* 18.

38. Saint John Damascene, PG 94:1340AB; see also Saint Theodore the Studite, PG 99:501BC.

39. Meyendorff, *Byzantine Theology, op. cit.,* p. 46.

40. PG 100:1113AB.

41. PG 94:1249CD.

42. PG 94:1252BD.

43. PG 98:181D.

44. PG 98:149B.

45. John Damascene, PG 94:1248CD.

46. PG 94:1245B.

47. PG 94:1245BC. See also PG 94:1300BC.

48. PG 98:185C. See also John Damascene, PG 94:1352D.

49. Nicephorus of Constantinople, PG 100:385AB; also Ouspensky in *Threskevtike kai ethike Egkyklopaideia* [Religious and Ethical Encyclopedia], 5:410.

Image, Symbol and Language
in Relation to the Holy Trinity

SOME PRELIMINARY REMARKS*

THE RELATION BETWEEN *fides* and *ratio* has been a constantly recurring theme throughout the long ages of Christian thought. Already Paul makes a sharp distinction between "the wisdom of this world" and "the wisdom of God in a mystery, even the hidden wisdom" (1 Cor. 2:6–7). "The hidden wisdom" and "the wisdom of this world" constitute two diametrically opposing realities and ways. They represent two extreme possibilities of seeing the beginning and the end, the existence and the *raison d'être* both of man and of the entire world.

"The hidden wisdom" is a wisdom taken captive by the power of God or, to put it differently, "the hidden wisdom" is God himself, "in whom are hid all the treasures of wisdom and knowledge" (Col. 2:2–3). "My speech," writes Paul to the Corinthians, "and my preaching was not with enticing words of man's wisdom, but in demonstration of the Spirit and of power: That your faith should not stand in the wisdom of men, but in the power of God" (1 Cor. 2:4–5).[1] The wisdom "of this world" is a wisdom held captive by human reason. Again we may look at the point from a different perspective. The wisdom of this world is a wisdom absolutely alien to God. Those who base their existence on it are described as walking "in the vanity of their mind, having their understanding darkened, being alienated from the life of God" (Eph. 4:17–18). In the epistle of James, we find a strong affirmation concerning human wisdom: "This wisdom descendeth not from above, but is earthly, sensual, devilish" (Jas. 3:15).

The aim of this paper is not to discuss the relationship between the wisdom of God based on faith and the wisdom of this world based on human reason, but to demonstrate how and to what extent "the hidden wisdom" can be grasped by human beings. The question is how the unutterable can be uttered. Or to look at the question from another angle, do we have the possibility of bringing to utterance what, in fact, is beyond human understanding? The question is not a new one: Plato had already made the statement that it is difficult to apprehend the Creator and the Father of this world, but to express Him is indeed an impossibility.[1] Saint Gregory the Theologian, referring to Plato without naming him, alters his statement and emphasizes that "to form an adequate concept of God is even more impossible than to express it when formed". The reason is because "that which may be apprehended may perhaps be expressed by language, if not relatively well at any rate imperfectly".[2]

For Orthodox patristic thought it is of primary and capital importance for any theological discussion to understand that the divine nature or essence is far beyond any knowledge, and consequently all human linguistic expression is absolutely inadequate. The supraessential nature cannot be a subject of human knowability. "God", points out Saint John of Damascus, "is infinite and incomprehensible, and all that is comprehensible about Him is His infinity and incomprehensibility. All that we say about God cataphatically does not show forth His nature but the things that are related to His nature."[3] This perspective of Saint

John of Damascus represents the foundation of the theological gnosiology of the entire patristic approach.

There is a remarkable consensus among the Greek fathers that what we know of God is not His ineffable nature, but His uncreated energies. We know God through his "manifestations" (ἐκφάνσεις), his "movement" (κίνησις), his "power" (δύναμις), his "bursting forth" (ἐξάλματα). "We know God," says Saint Basil the Great, "by his energies, but we do not assert that we can approach his essence; his energies descend to us, although his nature remains unapproachable."[4]

It is true and has been admitted on all sides that one of the fundamental points of patristic theological gnosiology is that the limited knowability of the divine energies and actions, as well as the absolute incomprehensibility of God's nature, do not form a kind of philosophical speculation, but rather presuppose an attitude, a personal experience of the revelation.[5]

This personal experience of the revelation is understood in terms of participation in the uncreated glory of God. In other words, the attitude of which we are speaking is not a knowledge, in a narrow and speculative sense of the term, but a way toward deification. This attitude presupposes a radical change of mentality. The term used in Greek is *metanoia* which means both "change of mind" or "reversal of the intellect" and "repentance". Bearing this in mind, we reach the conclusion that this attitude leads to a knowledge which is, in fact, a radical transformation of human wisdom, a wisdom which is called by Paul, "Foolishness of the message preached" (μωρία τοῦ κηρύγματος, 1 Cor. 1:21). It is of paramount importance to understand that Christian theology, in order to be genuine, must be a destruction of "the wisdom of the wise" (1 Cor. 1:19; *cf.* Isa. 29:14). One has to elevate one's self from the level of "natural" ways of thinking to the level of contempla-tion of the mysteries revealed. On this level, theology, prayer and communion with God are not simply in close connection but are, in fact, interwoven. They constitute one and the same reality: a state where the human person is dominated and illuminated by God in such a way that his theological language is brought to its true essence. The unknown author of the fifth century in the prologue of his treatise on *The Mystical Theology* describes this "captured by God" attitude:

Supernal Triad, Deity above all essence, Knowledge and Goodness; Guide of Christians to Divine Wisdom; Direct our path to the ultimate summit of Thy mystical Love, most incomprehensible, most luminous and most exalted, where the pure, absolute and immutable mysteries of theology are veiled in the dazzling obscurity of the secret Silence, outshining all brilliance with the intensity of their Darkness, and surcharging our blinded intellects with the utterly impalpable and invisible fairness of glories surpassing all beauty.[6]

From all this it is not surprising, therefore, to observe that to speak about God presupposes the acceptance of both the priority of revelation and the faithfulness of those theologizing; not to the natural concepts of the human mind, but to an attitude which is based on love and communion. It is significant that according to Saint Gregory of Nyssa, knowledge of God and communion or participation in God are bound together. More than that, knowledge of God and communion with God are explicitly considered as identical (γνῶσις δὲ κατὰ τὸ ἐγχωροῦν ἐστιν ἡ μετουσία).[7] The process of love and communion leads to a personal experience of revelation that enables the human person to know God and to use true theological language, a language which will never be "a bastard form of speech",[8] working through speculations and purely human categories, but through contemplation.

Christian theology in the final and ultimate analysis is not the reflections of an individual, but arises within the ecclesial community. It is in the Church, this place of love and communion, that theology can attain its fullness and its true essence, given that the God of the Christians is not the impersonal supreme Being of the philosophers. It has been rightly said that the way of existence of the Church is an image and reflection of the way in which God exists.[9] This means that each human person in the Church is an "image" of God in the sense that he exists in communion as God himself exists in communion.

The fact that the way of existence of the Church is an image of the way of God's existence, and that in the Church each human being is understood as an image of God, is significant for the understanding of theology itself. The *Imago Dei* ecclesiology and anthropology represent a solid basis upon which one can build an "image theology". In other words, one cannot see the symbolic and iconic character of Christian theology unless one understands the Church's mode of existence as an image of God's existence, that is to say, as a communion, and unless one sees the human person as an image of God's reality.

The human person as an image of God in the Church, which herself is also an image of God,[10] becomes a "receptacle receiving goods" (χώρημα δεκτικῶν ἀγαθῶν),[11] he partakes of God and as such has something akin (συγγενές) to that in which he participates. As an image of God, he is endowed with life, reason, wisdom and all the divine goods, so that by each of them, he is directed toward his archetype.[12]

This clearly means that one's way of thinking and one's way of speaking about God are not based on a subject–object principle, but on a completely new reality-relation, that of the ecclesial communion. It is evident that by entering into this communion one is not only a participant in the divine glory, but is also united to others who share this common knowledge and life. Thus, within the ecclesial body every human person shares through *ascesis*[13] a common and identical experience. Consequently one shares the same theology and makes one's own the same method; and thus one understands the iconic language and the symbols used by all persons who have experienced or are now experiencing the event of the ecclesial communion.

We have to emphasize here that ecclesial communion as the sole and adequate foundation of the common experience is the basis of unity in truth. This means that the same faith – the understanding of the faith as well as the expression of that faith – is only possible within the ecclesial body. The iconic and symbolic language which characterizes the Christian way of speaking about God has its own context, and this is the context of the *corpus Christi*. Outside this reality icons and symbols appear simply as mythological descriptions. It is my personal conviction that the well known "De-mythologizing program" of Bultmann and his school was ambiguous and, consequently, misleading for the simple reason that it was based on the principle of individualistic analysis, outside of any living context, and that images referring to God were evaluated in purely human terms and categories. It is not my intention here to enter into a dialogue with this school. But it seems to me very important for our investigation to make clear that, for any understanding of iconic and symbolic language when speaking about God, the individual must transcend individuality and enter into the catholic consciousness of the Church. Otherwise, one can fall into a rationalization of the Church's iconic-symbolic language.

In this connection something must be added to clarify the great distinction between symbolic language and conceptual language. The point we have already made is that the only adequate language one can use when speaking about God is a symbolic and iconic language. This is because concepts about God presuppose that He can be reduced to an object of human investigation and analysis. In such a case God is understood as one reality among many others or, in the best case, as being above the others of this world. But if we accept the image of God given by Christian faith, that is to say, if we recognize that God is not limited to the finite world, then conceptual language becomes an imperfect organ to express His reality. In fact abstract conceptions concerning God transform Christian theology into metaphysics. This means, in other words, that purely "conceptual theology" is a distortion of Christian theology in that it operates as a rationalization of the Christian faith, reducing God to an object of analysis.[14]

By contrasting symbolic and conceptual language as we have, and claiming that it is only through symbolic language that we can properly speak about the Triune God, we do not intend either to over-emphasize the part that symbols play in theology or to under-value and absolutely disconnect human reason in the theological process. We must make this more precise by clarifying certain points.

The use of symbols, icons, parables and metaphors is fundamental to the scriptural approach to divine revelation. It is the language of the prophets, the "teaching method" of our Lord, God and Saviour Jesus Christ, and the foundation of the apostolic interpretation of Christ, his mission and the Church. Thus it is a divinely inspired given of any authentic approach to Christian theology.

By using symbols, icons, and so forth, when speaking of God, we simply recognize that we cannot give a purely rational explanation of God's existence, of his inner-Trinitarian life and of his relationship to the world. In other words, symbols and icons are not used in purely theological discussion[15] as a kind of trinitarian speculation; they do not play the role of theoretical statements and definitions. Thus, they are not used to replace concepts. The rationalization of symbols is equally excluded from Orthodox theology, as is the absolutizing of human reason. This means that symbols as well as human reason have their own limitations. On the other hand, symbols are not symbols in the narrow sense. They are not simply and only symbols. From an Orthodox patristic viewpoint, symbols are directly connected with truth. Symbols and icons represent something which exists, something "real"[16] and not something imaginary.

This was, in fact, the Orthodox response during the long iconoclastic controversy. Saint John of Damascus makes a clear distinction between "shadow" and "image". Basing himself on Hebrews 10:1,[17] he comments that image represents a complete reality. Contrasted with the Law, which is a "preliminary sketch for a picture" (προχάραγμα) and a "shadow" (σκιά or προσκίασμα) of "the good things to come", the New Testament presents to us the very image of those things.[18] It is in Christ and in the Church of Christ that image represents truth. In the Church, truth is in no way understood as an intellectual construct, as a metaphysical concept, built upon a philosophical foundation, but as a reality in which to *participate.* The defenders of the veneration of icons during the iconoclastic controversy did not support a particular theological method among many others, neither did they argue for a theological comprehension. They struggled rather to preserve the unique Christian tradition which understands theology as a vision, an event in which one participates, manifested as an epiphany in the Church and through the methods set forth by the Church. The fathers of the second Council of Nicaea (787) were deeply aware that icons and symbols protect truth from any rationalization and objectification. They keep the way clear for a direct, existential (not individualistic), communal and participatory vision of truth.

Let us now briefly examine certain concrete examples of the symbolic and iconic language used in the New Testament and the Christian tradition, to see their significance and function. We shall limit our exposition to the symbols and icons related to the Trinitarian mystery.

Studying the New Testament data as well as those of Christian history, we find that symbols and images used to express in some way the reality of the Triune God are taken from two sources. The one is the so-called "natural" world[19] and the other is the human state or world.[20] We have to observe that by using symbols and images from the natural world, the risk of rationalization is to a great extent limited – not eliminated, but certainly limited. There is a kind of distance between man and the natural world, so that man can easily see the limits and functions of symbols and images based on its realities. When, for example, we speak of God as "Light" (Luke 2:32; John 1:7–9, and so forth), the symbolism is so clear that no one would identify light and God. The same is true when we speak of God as "fountain" (Rev. 21:6). Again the symbolism is evident, and no one would think to reverse the statement and say that the fountain is God. But when we use symbols and images derived from human experience, the danger of rationalization is always present, given that man is existentially involved in the human and historic situation. Thus, often one confuses or identifies symbols and images related to God with symbols and images related to one's own human life. This was, for example, the case of Arius, who understood "generation", "fatherhood" and "sonship" in human terms. Consequently, he denied the eternity of the Logos of God, and held that he is not true God, but rather a creature whom the Father formed out of nothing as the beginning and agent of his creation.

But it would be a serious misunderstanding to place the image of generation and sonship within an anthropomorphic context and identify the eternal generation and sonship of the Logos of God with human generation and sonship. It is beyond doubt that in Christian theology the categories of fatherhood, generation and sonship have a unique and peculiar significance. This means that the images of fatherhood and sonship, when related to the Triune God, are not derived from human experience. In other words, human and divine fatherhood are two absolutely incomparable realities. Likewise, the sonship of the Logos of God cannot be understood and interpreted in human terms. The "sonship of our Saviour", writes Alexander of Alexandria, "has absolutely no communion with the sonship of human persons."[21]

This means that in Christian theology divine fatherhood and sonship transcend human fatherhood and sonship. Any attempt to limit our understanding of the fatherhood or sonship of God to human models leads to an anthropomorphic understanding of God and, consequently, to a theology confined within the narrow framework of human reason. In such a case there is no room for a theology of faith, nor for a theology based on common ecclesial experience and vision.

Early Christian writers and, more specifically, the fathers of the First Ecumenical Council, in order to avoid anthropomorphism and to clarify the Orthodox teaching concerning the relationship between God the Father and the eternal Logos of God, as well as the nature of that unique relationship, used a biblical image derived from the natural world: that of "Light". The image had already been used in the Old Testament in reference to God, but the Evangelist John at the beginning of his Gospel uses it to focus attention on the deity of the Logos:

There was a man sent from God, whose name was John. The same came for a witness, to bear witness of the Light, that all men through him might believe. He was not that Light, but was sent to bear witness of that Light. That was the true Light, which lighteth every man that cometh into the world (John 1:6–9).

"Light" as a theological symbol can be analysed in many ways and can illustrate several aspects of Christian theology. Obviously we cannot here examine every instance of the use of this image. What we intend to do is to show in brief how this symbol was used as a hermeneutical key to illustrate the divinity of God's Logos and his eternal relation to the Father.

In the theological debate of the fourth century the consistent desire of the fathers was to demonstrate that there is a unique relation between the "one Lord Jesus Christ" and the "one God the Father". The goal of the fathers was to illustrate that the New Testament affirmations that Christ was "in the beginning *with* God the Father" (John 1:1–2; *cf.* 1 John 1:2), that he is *"in* the Father, and the Father *in* him" (*cf.* John 14:10, 20), and that he "was sent" *by* the Father (*e.g.* John 3:37; 7:29), designate the central Christian truth that Jesus Christ is God's only begotten Son. These biblical expressions affirm that the Father and the Son inhere and coexist eternally, that is to say, "timelessly" (ἀχρόνως) and "unoriginately" (ἀνάρχως).[22]

It was to counter the anthropomorphic understanding of "Fatherhood," "Sonship" and "generation" that the Nicene fathers used the image of "Light", and formulated the expression "Light from Light", which they included in the Nicene-Constantinopolitan Creed. The use of this biblical symbol enabled them to protect Christian theology from the intrusion of anthropomorphic elements, that is to say, from any corporeal or creaturely overtones and implications. The point is very simple, and was explained clearly and on numerous occasions by Saint Athanasius.[23] Light is always connected with its radiance. Where no radiance exists, no light exists. This means that the Father is never without the Son. Where the Father is, the Son is also. As it is unthinkable to separate the light from its radiance, so it is unthinkable to see the Father without his only-begotten Son. There is something common between the light and its radiance, such that one cannot think of the one without thinking at the same time of the other. Likewise, between the Father and the Son there is no interval in being; but there is eternal and harmonious mutuality.[24] Thus Christ is the unique, the natural and true Son of the Father. He is "the express image of the Father's ὑπόστασις and Light from Light, and true Power and Image of the Being of the Father".[25]

The Nicene clause "Light from Light" as a theological paradigm protects, as we have already noted, the ineffable relation between the Father and the Son and, at the same time, indicates that this relation transcends and exceeds human capacity, given that it is not merely by analogy with physical light that God is called "Light".[26]

We note here that in the tradition of the Eastern Church "Light theology" is not a theoretical chapter of her doctrine, but has a profound significance, and consequently has influenced her whole life. Thus the feast of Theophany, on which the Church celebrates the manifestation of the Holy Trinity on the occasion of Christ's baptism and the illumination of the whole world by the light of the incarnate Logos, is also called the "Feast of Lights". It is also significant that the earliest fathers maintained as an apostolic tradition that all Christian prayer must be said facing East, the direction from which springs the Sun of righteousness (Mal. 4:2), the pre-eternal Light, Christ our God. Even the martyrs were careful in their final prayers before their death to observe this ancient precept, thus showing in popular and practical terms that the understanding of Christ as Light from Light is no abstract construct.

One could add that the image of "Light" in relation to the holy Trinity is frequently used in Eastern hymnology. This can clearly be seen in two hymns. The first is one of the earliest surviving examples of Christian hymnology (before the fourth century), the well-known "Gladsome" or "Joyful Light . . . " (Φῶς ἱλαρόν). The other example is a hymn (*exaposteilarion*) from the feast of the Transfiguration of Christ.

O joyful Light of the holy glory of the immortal Father, heavenly, holy, blessed, Jesus Christ: now that we are come to the setting of the sun and behold the evening light, we sing in praise to God the Father, Son, and Holy Spirit. It is meet at all times to praise Thee in hymns with happy voice, O Son of God, who grantest life: therefore, the world gives Thee glory.

Today on Tabor in the manifestation of thy Light, O Word, Thou unaltered Light from the Light of the unbegotten Father, we have seen the Father as Light and the Son as Light, guiding with Light the whole creation.[27]

Anthropomorphic theology as an incorrect use of theological images was always a temptation for Christian theology. Man in his attempt to speak about God, living within his own human and historic situation, often used metaphors and figures of speech which have low and corporeal ingredients. As a classic example, one can mention the image of the Holy Trinity introduced and widely used in the Middle Ages. This image represents God the Father as an old man seated on a throne; on his right is seated Christ, carrying his cross. The Holy Spirit in the form of a dove is placed in the middle and above them. It is evident that this extremely anthropomorphic representation of the Holy Trinity is as incompatible with Orthodox theology as the rationalization of trinitarian doctrine. G. Aulén, in his study concerning symbols, makes the observation that anthropomorphism and rationalization "are inclined to go together".[28]

An icon is never a copy based on a human model or derived from the painter's imagination. An icon is never constrained by the characteristics of this world and, obviously, is not an autonomous reality, but is connected and subordinated to the Church's tradition. It conveys and expresses the life of the Church. The icon is a part of the worship of the Church; it is substantially interwoven with her whole experience, thus revealing to the faithful the invisible through the visible.

Bearing this in mind, we can understand why Orthodoxy has constantly refused – in spite of certain abuses of the last few centuries due to scholastic influences – to produce an icon of the Holy Trinity based on anthropomorphic principles. The Orthodox Church, faithful to the decisions of the Seventh Ecumenical Council, emphasized the absolute impossibility of representing God the Father.[29] Saint Theodore the Studite makes the comment that "since he was born of the indescribable Father, [Christ] cannot have an image. Indeed, what image could correspond to the divinity whose representation is absolutely forbidden by Holy Scripture? But from the moment Christ is born of a describable mother, he naturally has an image which corresponds to that of his mother. If he could not be represented by art, this would mean that he was not born of a representable mother, but that he was born only of the Father, and that he was not incarnate. But this contradicts the whole divine economy of our salvation."[30]

For the Orthodox, the refusal to produce an icon of the Holy Trinity based on anthropomorphic principles does not signify that the Church is opposed to any symbolic representation of it. Leonid Ouspensky points out that:

We only represent what has been revealed to us: the incarnate person of the Son of God, Jesus Christ. The Holy Spirit is represented as It manifested Itself: in the shape of a dove at the baptism of Christ, in the form of tongues of fire at Pentecost, and so on. As for God the Father, His presence is only indicated symbolically in icons: usually a blessing hand is represented coming from heaven, this in general indicating the divine presence.[31]

But undoubtedly for the Orthodox tradition the icon *par excellence* of the Holy Trinity is the icon of the hospitality of Abraham. The three angels of the Old Testament story (Gen. 18: 1 ff) represent in a purely symbolic manner the three divine persons. Without any anthropomorphism, this icon of the Holy Trinity points out what is in fact beyond man's grasp: the Divine, the Supreme Reality.

It has already been stated and must again be underscored that outside the Church symbolic and iconic language becomes an "empty deceit", a mere and sterile philosophical speculation, leading nowhere. It is only within the Church that one understands symbols, icons and theological language, not as products of the mind or of human experience, but as a means of communion and as witnesses and visions of truth. Thus, when we speak of symbolism, we presuppose that this symbolism is ecclesiological, in the sense that symbols and icons have an apocalyptic character only within the Church. The Church, as the image of divine communion and the prefiguration and foretaste of the perfect communion in a transfigured earth and new heaven, is the place where images and symbols carry a revelatory message – a message about God, from God.

NOTES

*A paper given at the Anglican–Orthodox International Commission held in Toronto, in September 1990. First published in *St. Vladimir's Theological Quarterly* 36 (1992), 257–271.

1. Plato, *Timaeus* 28c.

2. *Theological Oration* II, 4 (*Oration* 28), ed. A. J. Mason, pp. 26–27; PG 36:29C. For a general introduction on the theme of the relation between the knowledge of God and theology in Cappadocian thought, see my work, *The Meaning of the Terms "Theology", "to Theologize", and "Theologian" in the Teaching of the Greek Fathers up to and Including the Cappadocians* (Athens, 1972), p. 163 ff [in Greek].

3. *On the Orthodox Faith* I, 4, ed. B. Kotter, p. 13; PG 94:800B.

4. *Epistle 234, To Amphilochius,* ed. Y. Courtonne, III, p. 42; PG 32:869AB. For a detailed discussion of this theme see, V. Lossky, *The Mystical Theology of the Eastern Church* (Crestwood NY, 1991), p. 67 ff.

5. For further discussion see Lossky, *op. cit.,* pp. 42–43. See also J. S. Romanides, "Critical examination of the applications of Theology", *Procès Verbaux du Deuxième Congrès de Théologie Orthodoxe* (Athens, 1978), p. 427.

6. PG 3:997AB. Eng. trans. the editors of The Shrine of Wisdom, *Mystical Theology and the Celestial Hierarchies by Dionysius the Areopagite* (Finty, [1949]), p. 9.

7. *On the Untimely Death of Infants,* PG 46:176B.

8. This expression is from E. Jüngel. See J. B. Webster, *Eberhard Jüngel. An Introduction to his Theology* (Cambridge, 1986), p. 42.

9. J. D. Zizioulas, *Being as Communion* (Crestwood NY, 1985), p. 15.

10. Ἐστὶ οὖν ἡ Ἐκκλησία τύπος καὶ εἰκὼν τοῦ Θεοῦ, Maximus the Confessor, *Mystagogy,* PG 91:705A.

11. Saint Gregory of Nyssa, *On the Soul and the Resurrection,* PG 46:105AB.

12. Saint Gregory of Nyssa, *Cathechetical Oration* 5, ed. J. H. Srawley, p. 23:10–15; PG 45:21D.

13. We use the term *ascesis* here in a broad sense, including therein prayer, fasting, almsgiving and, in general, every personal devotion realized within the life of the Church.

14. A most interesting discussion of the theme "concept of God and image of God" can be found in G. Aulén, *The Drama and the Symbols: A Book on Images of God and the Problems They Raise,* Eng. trans. S. Linton (London, 1970), pp. 90–95.

15. When we speak here of "theological discussion", we refer to the teaching concerning the Triune God as distinct from the teaching concerning his economy and his relationship with creation.

16. "Accustomed to an idea of reality determined by rationalism and historicism, we tend to consider as 'truths' and 'facts' the things which experience verifies or which correspond to certain norms and concepts 'grasped' by us as true . . . The use of the term εἰκών does not signify this kind of factual truth, nor any lack of reality. For all the Greek fathers, except those of the Origenist school, εἰκών always means something *real* and as true as ἀλήθεια," Zizioulas, *op. cit.,* p. 99.

17. "For the law having a shadow of good things to come, and not the very image of the things, can never with those sacrifices which they offered year by year continually make the comers thereunto perfect."

18. *On the Divine Images* I, 15, ed. Kotter, p. 88; PG 94:1244D–1245A.

19. For example, God is called "Light". Thus James points out that "Every good gift and every perfect gift is from above, and cometh down from the Father of lights, with whom is no variableness, neither shadow of turning" (Jas. 1:17). John also in his first epistle states, "This then is the message which we have heard of him, and declare unto you, that God is light, and in him is no darkness at all" (1 John 1:5). God is also described as "heaven". Thus in the Gospel of Matthew we find Christ's question to the chief priest of the Temple: "The baptism of John, whence was it? from heaven, or of men?" (Matt. 21:25). The notion "heaven" as synonymous with God is also used by John the Baptist, who said that "A man can receive nothing, except it be given him from heaven" (John 3:27).

20. For example, God is called "King". He is the "King of kings" (Rev. 19:16). He is "the King eternal, immortal, invisible" (1 Tim. 1:17). He is also the "Lord" (see for example Matt. 22:37; Luke 19:38). The symbols "Father" and "Son" have in the New Testament their specific meaning, indicating the two divine persons. We see this clearly in Christ's injunction to his disciples: "Go ye therefore, and teach all nations, baptizing them in the name of the Father, and of the Son, and of the Holy Ghost" (Matt. 28:19).

21. *Letter to Alexander of Constantinople* VII (PG 18:557C).

22. Gregory the Theologian, *Oration* 30, 11 and 19; PG 36:116C and 128C.

23. See for example. *On the Decrees of the Council of Nicaea* 24, 2; 25, 2; 27, 2, ed. H. G. Opitz, pp. 20, 21, 23; PG 25:457C and 460C; *Against the Arians* I, 24; PG 26:61BC; *Against the Gentiles* 46, 50–61, ed. R. W. Thomson, p. 130; PG 25:93BC.

24. For an illuminating discussion on this theme, see T. F. Torrance, *The Trinitarian Faith: The Evangelical Theology of the Ancient Catholic Church* (Edinburgh, 1988), p. 119 ff.

25. *Contra Arianos,* I, 9, quoted by T. F. Torrance, *op. cit.,* p. 121.

26. Gregory Palamas, *Against Akindynus* (*Argument 1a*); PG 150:823, quoted by Lossky, *op. cit.,* p. 220.

27. I use the translations from the original Greek by Mother Mary and Archimandrite Kallistos Ware, *The Festal Menaion* (London, 1969), pp. 83 and 495.

28. See Aulén, *op. cit.,* p. 136.

29. For a further discussion, see L. Ouspensky, *Theology of the Icon* (Crestwood NY, 1978), p. 183 ff.

30. Saint Theodore the Studite, *Third Refutation,* Chapter II, PG 99:417C. Quoted by Ouspensky, *op. cit.,* p. 182.

31. *Ibid.,* pp. 183–184.

Holy Scripture and Councils*

HOLY SCRIPTURE IS THE BOOK of the Christian community. Firstly, because it is addressed to the faithful, the members of the Christian community: Holy Scripture is created for the Church. This means that it is created so that the Church may be preserved in the continuity of a revelatory reality, a life which the Apostles received and transmitted, and which constitutes the final purpose and meaning of man's existence. "But these are written, that ye might believe that Jesus is the Christ, the Son of God; and that believing ye might have life through his name" (John 20:31). There is a clear and specific purpose which justifies the existence of Holy Scripture: "that ye might believe that Jesus is the Christ, the Son of God". Holy Scripture is the word of God concerning that which "Jesus did in the presence of his disciples" (John 20:30); it is the very life-bearing word of the Lord and the Apostles preserved to the ages. Holy Scripture constitutes the written, authentic rendering of the divine message and the unshakeable proof of the *kenosis* of the Word of God and the unique events of salvation which are unceasingly offered in the Church. Further, Holy Scripture constitutes the greatest proof that whatever we do today is not the product of man's thought; it does not hang, as it were, suspended in mid-air, but is firmly based upon the mystery of Christ and the experience of the Apostolic Church.[1]

In the Bible, God reveals himself and bears witness to himself for the edification of the faithful and for the salvation of the world. Thus, Holy Scripture as a whole, offered to the Church, is not simply and exclusively a book of the Christian community, but a book of the Christian community with catholic and ecumenical dimensions. It is offered to the Church for the edification of the people of God, but it is at the very same time a book through which the Church enters into dialogue with the world. This means that Holy Scripture is the missionary book of the Christian community. It has a dual purpose: the edification and the increase of the people of God. Through Holy Scripture, God reveals himself to the Church, and through the Church to the world. In other words, Holy Scripture is a revelatory reality. Indeed, throughout the Bible, revelation which has been completed by God through the Apostles becomes a continuous present in the Church, and through the Church is conveyed to the world. Through the Bible the Church lives, throughout all the phases of her history, the life that the Apostles transmitted, and she is continuously rebaptized in those divine laws which the Apostles themselves enacted in accordance with a revelation transmitted for the salvation of the world. That is to say, Holy Scripture does not simply speak of a certain history, but rather is itself a living history, able to change the already spoken words of the Lord into words of life, into a continuous presence of the Saviour. The Apostles, recording the events of the life and work of Christ, did not perform simply an act of historiography. They were not writers of history in the usual sense of the term, but preachers of the mystery of life and salvation.[2] "For the life was manifested, and we have seen it, and bear witness, and show unto you that eternal life, which was with the Father, and was manifested unto us" (1 John 1:2). They had as a starting point the mystery of Pentecost, through which they saw all the aspects of the life of the historical Jesus and his work in another, new light. Holy Scripture, created for the Church, transmits this new light to the faithful community.

Holy Scripture is begotten *for* the Church but also *in* the Church. This means that the Bible in its totality is a creation of the community. Both in the Old Testament and in the New, it is the community that shows forth the sacred books. Indeed, it is a known fact that the Church had before herself many more historical, legal and other texts than those which she finally chose and considered as canonical. The Church being "the pillar and ground of the truth" (1 Tim. 3:15) and "filled with the Holy Trinity",[3] proceeds to choose those works which had already been acknowledged by use, chiefly liturgical, within the ecclesiastical community.[4] This choosing is a kind of seal. The Church chooses those texts which have been inter-woven into her life. She chooses, from a multitude of texts, those which are divinely inspired, while she rejects others as "apocryphal" or characterizes them as "deuterocanonical". Holy Scripture was given to the Church and the Church transmits it to the people as the authentic written rendition of the life-bearing message, which the incarnate Logos brought for the re-creation of all creation. The Church in defining the canon of Holy Scripture accepts and bears within herself "the Word of truth". "The Word of truth" is acknowledged by the believing community, by the entire body of Christ. It is not an isolated and autonomous principle, alien to the Church. Holy Scripture and the Church cannot be separated. One is contained in the other *(perichoresis),* one depends upon the other. Holy Scripture is created for the Church and the Church is the basis for its genesis.

Those who separate Holy Scripture from the Church come to the false conclusion that either Scripture is superior to the Church or that the Church is superior to Holy Scripture. The first opinion one finds among Protestant theologians, while the latter is to be found in Roman Catholic theology. This hyperbole leads to an alteration of the meaning of the Church, that is, either to an under-evaluation (subordination) or to an over-evaluation. By placing the Bible over and above the Church we destroy the balance, we corrupt its canonical position, and take the first step towards an "individualistic" theology, outside the Church. On the other hand, the idea that the Church is superior to Holy Scripture leads to the opinion that the Church is able to draw from herself every dogma. Only if we accept that the Church and Scripture are neither separated nor confused, being united without confusion (ἀσυγχύτως ἡνωμέναι) will we be able to understand that the Church alone is she who can find the true meaning of Holy Scripture, just as the Son alone is he who is able to understand the words of the Father.[5]

It is not by chance and not without meaning that in the Orthodox Church the community invoke divine aid in order to understand the Scriptures. In every Divine Liturgy before the reading of the Gospel, the priest prays: "O Merciful Master, cause the pure light of the knowledge of thee to shine in our hearts, and open the eyes of our mind to perceive the proclamation of thy Gospel".[6] Scripture cannot be approached by reading but by understanding, and this understanding is wrought through the Church. The Church opens the path towards understanding and the Church has the power to open this road because she does not base herself upon human judgment but upon the original apostolic interpretation. In other words, in the Church, Holy Scripture is interpreted and understood through Tradition. By saying that in Orthodoxy the Bible is interpreted and understood through Tradition, we mean that the Apostles through the Church interpret themselves. This is so simply because the Apostles, along with and parallel to the Scriptures, left Tradition to the Church, in order to safeguard their teaching.[7] It is precisely this Tradition, kept alive through the energy of the Holy Spirit, that interprets Holy Scripture and is interpreted by Holy Scripture.

In the Eastern Orthodox Church the subject of "Tradition" is of capital importance. It is within this subject that the question of the Councils should be examined. Saint Paul already refers to the significance of Tradition: "Therefore, brethren, stand fast, and hold the traditions which ye have been taught, whether by word, or our epistle" (2 Thess. 2:15). Tradition, in the same way as Scripture, is given to the Church as the word of life. And the Church, the entire body of Christ, preserves Tradition and refers to it exactly as it refers to the Holy Scriptures. The Church appears as a continuous synod, spread out in time and space, but constantly vigilant, and always active, in order to express the truth being experienced within her own Tradition; always prepared to interpret the word of faith which is rooted in the Holy Scriptures, and which is then interpreted through Tradition. Holy Scripture offers the seeds which the Church as a universal (catholic) synod interprets through her Tradition.

The meaning of the Church as a continuous and living synod refers to its essence, and this is already declared from the time of the Apostles during the first *synaxes* for the celebration of the Holy Eucharist. Indeed the whole Church, under the Apostles, clergy and laymen, participated in such sacramental assemblies of the people of God, in which the totality of the Church, animated by the spirit of unity and love and convoked by the Holy Spirit, constitutes a constant, ecumenical and living synod.[8] This continuous synod of the people of God has as its indestructible foundation "the holy synod" of the *zoarchic* and life-giving Trinity, convoked by God the Father, through Jesus Christ, in the Holy Spirit, and henceforth convoked uninterruptedly as a Eucharistic *synaxis* under the bishop (the living image of Christ, and even of God the Father himself, according to both Ignatius the God-bearer and Symeon of Thessalonica),[9] who offers to God in Trinity the Divine Eucharist, the body of Christ, in which all believers are united, and of which they are communicants.[10] The Church, therefore, for which and from which Holy Scripture is born is herself a synod.

More specifically, the principles of the synodical system go back to the election of Matthias by the Apostles and the other disciples with them, who "were about an hundred and twenty" (Acts 1:15 ff), and also to the election of the seven deacons (Acts 6:2 ff). In these elections one can clearly discern conciliar characteristics; but most especially it is in the Apostolic Council of Jerusalem (Acts 15:6 ff) that the participation of the totality of the Church is apparent. During this Council, in order to take a decision, "the apostles and elders came together for to consider of this matter" (Acts 15:6). Compare also the following verses: "Then pleased it the apostles and elders, with the whole church" (Acts 15:22); "It seemed good unto us, being assembled with one accord" (Acts 15:25); "For it seemed good to the Holy Ghost, and to us" (Acts 15:28). Just as the Holy Scriptures are given to the totality of the Church as a revealed reality in order that the Church be preserved in the continuity of the new life in Christ, so is the Council given to the catholic Church as a right belonging to all the people of God, so that they can bear witness, when necessary, to the holy character of the revelation and safeguard the dogmatic truths. At the Council, the totality of the Church is present, by virtue of the harmonic and absolute agreement of all the members of the one and only body – no juridical discrimination exists between clergy and lay members.

Certainly the rapid growth of the Church has rendered much more obvious the special *charisma* of the bishops to represent each his own Church. However, such a representation presupposes the unity of the people of God, which *as a totality* constitutes the ultimate criterion of the ecumenicity of a Council. Every decision, be it of dogmatic or canonical character, must be ratified by the "yes" of the people of the Church, must be interwoven with the life of the body, must become the flesh and blood of the Church. It is only thus that a Council may be called "ecumenical", and its word considered of equal value to that of the apostolic seed.

It is precisely this *pleroma* or the whole body of the Church – constituted by all who believe in the orthodox way, clerics and lay persons – that is considered in Orthodoxy as the bearer of the infallibility of the Church; while as the voice of the Church and the instrument for the expression of this infallibility we have the supreme authority, that is to say the Ecumenical Council, in which the *pleroma* of the Church, represented by its bishops, dogmatize through the energy, guidance and inspiration of the Holy Spirit.[11]

It is this reality of the people of God that constitutes the point of convergence between Holy Scripture and the Ecumenical

Councils. The Bible was born for the Church and within the Church; and the Councils were also born for the Church and within the Church. Just as the Church herself, when determining the New Testament canon, selects those texts that have been accepted by the community and have been acknowledged by the people of God, so too is this same principle operative as regards the Councils, where the totality of the body of the Church expresses its conscience and faith, that which it has lived and experienced from the very beginning; that is to say, the reality of the revelation which constitutes its own sustenance. The people of God itself preserves its faith, and for this very reason the decisions of the Councils are not imposed by means of monarchical powers, nor again are they ensured by a simple democratic vote, but they are always the product of the total faith of the Church; they express *quod ubique, quod semper, quod ab omnibus creditum est.* "The protector of religion is the body of the Church itself, namely the people itself", clearly notes the encyclical of the Orthodox Patriarchs of the East of 1848.[12]

The ecumenicity of a Council is not given *a priori*; it does not depend on the number of the Council's participants or on the will of the convener, but upon its acceptance by the *corpus christianorurn,* in which the Paraclete acts and which it directs. In other words, it is the Holy Spirit who renders a Council Ecumenical and Catholic, and the people of God acknowledge this reality, that is, the primacy of the Holy Spirit. At the Councils the agreement among the Fathers was founded upon the inspiration of the Holy Spirit, and upon the truth that the Holy Spirit revealed. The certainty that the Holy Spirit was directing the work of the Councils, so that the Fathers of the Synod expressed the common conscience and faith of the Church, as well as the liturgical and spiritual experience of the whole *pleroma* of the Church, can be seen in the texts of the Councils themselves. The Council of Jerusalem declares categorically: "For it seemed good to the Holy Ghost, and to us" (Acts 15:28). Thenceforth this statement has constituted the Councils' golden rule.

Just as the authors of the books of Holy Scripture do not perform a work of historiography or chronography, but witness in the Holy Spirit to the mystery of salvation, so the Fathers of the Ecumenical Councils are not simple commentators but the "mystic trumpets of the Spirit", "those who sang the harmonious melody of theology in the midst of the Church"; they are those who "have consulted with the Holy Spirit", who rendered to the Church "the mystery of Theology".[13] Of course the Ecumenical Council does not stand above the Church; it is not a power over the Church, but serves the people of God, the Church from which it derives authority, prestige and infallibility. The Church stands above the Ecumenical Council; the Church uses the Ecumenical Council as an instrument for the interpretation of divine revelation. The Ecumenical Council is a supplication of the totality of the Church to the Spirit of truth, a cry of the whole body of the Church to the Paraclete, beseeching him to interpret Holy Scripture and Tradition. The Ecumenical Council is a community of seeking, searching, discovering and formulating the revealed truth, in which the totality of the body of the Church participates.[14]

NOTES

* This paper was first published in *Sobornost* 7 (1984), 111–116.

1. M. A. Siotis, "The Word of God", *The Living Logos*. A Spiritual Symposium on Holy Scripture (Athens, 1970), p. 27; D. Staniloae, "Holy Scripture in relation to the Church and Tradition", *ibid.*, p. 63 ff.

2. "Understand, then, the Gospel of Christ and the other divine Scriptures as being a container having eternal life locked and sealed within themselves, along with those ineffable, eternal good things which are invisible to our physical eyes", Symeon the New Theologian, On Spiritual Knowledge, *Homily* 24, 2.

3. Origen, *On Psalms* 23 (PG 12:1265B); J. N. Karmiris, *Orthodox Ecclesiology* (Athens, 1973), p. 199 ff [in Greek].

4. G. Florovsky, "Revelation and Interpretation", in *Bible, Church, Tradition: An Eastern Orthodox View* (Belmont MA, 1972), pp. 17–18; and P. Evdokimov, *L'Orthodoxie* (Neuchâtel, 1965), p. 189.

5. D. Staniloae, *op. cit.*, p. 83.

6. *The Divine Liturgy of Saint John Chrysostom.*

7. "We have received (Holy) Tradition from our Fathers as a legacy passed on from the Apostles and committed (to us) by the saints who followed", Gregory of Nyssa, *Against Eunomius* 4; ed. W. Jaeger, Vol. 2, p. 79; PG 45:653B; "Of the dogmas and kerygmata preserved in the Church, we possess some from written teaching, while we have received others from the Tradition of the apostles, which have reached us in mystery; both have equal force for piety", Saint Basil the Great, *On the Holy Spirit* (PG 32:188A ff); "We must also make use of Tradition: for it is impassible to take everything from Divine Scripture. For this reason the apostles transmitted some things by Scripture and other things by Tradition" (Saint Epiphanius of Salamis, *Against the Hereses* 61, 6; ed. K. Holl, GCS, Vol. 31 (Leipzig, 1915), p. 386; PG 41:1048B.

8. P. Evdokimov, *op. cit.*, p. 195.

9. For the bishop as image of Christ, see for example, *To the Smyrnaeans* 8, 2; and as image of the Father, see *To the Trallians* 3, 1; and in Symeon, see his *On the Priesthood* (PG 155:965AB), respectively.

10. J. N. Karmiris, "The Seven Ecumenical Councils and the Local Councils Ratified by Them". Paper submitted to the Joint Commission on Dialogue between Orthodox and Old Catholics at Chambésy (Athens, 1975), p. 1.

11. J. N. Karmiris, *Τὰ δογματικὰ καὶ συμβολικὰ μνημεῖα τῆς Ὀρθοδόξου Καθολικῆς Ἐκκλησίας* [The Dogmatic and Symbolic Monuments of the Orthodox Catholic Church], Vol. 1, 2 (Athens, 1960), pp. 106-107.

12. J. D. Mansi, *Sacrorum Conciliorum Nova et Amplissima Collectio*, Vol. 40 (Graz, 1909 repr. ed.), p. 407.

13. From the hymnology of the Orthodox Church.

14. D. Staniloae, *op. cit.*, pp. 90-91.

Paradosis

THE ORTHODOX UNDERSTANDING OF TRADITION*

THERE CAN BE NO DOUBT that we are living in a tragic world, a world embarked on a course with no end in sight, a path which seems to lead nowhere. It is to this world of ours, caught up in its own futility, that the Church comes to show another path, and she does this by projecting her own mode of existence. After all, was it not Christ who said "I am the way" (John 14:6)? Thus it is that the Church comes to pit against the tragedy of human history her own being, her own life. "For the life was manifested, and we have seen it, and bear witness, and shew unto you that eternal life, which was with the Father, and was manifested unto us" (1 John 1:2). Within the uncertainty of the contemporary world, the Church emerges as the only possibility for genuine life. The Church enters the universe as a "new cosmos", as the "creation of another world".[1]

Of course it is evident that when we speak of the Church we do not mean a social or a secular organism, or even a humanitarian society concerned with the moral betterment of human life. By Church we mean the life-giving Body of the God-Man: we mean Christ himself transmitted and extended to the ages. In the final analysis, when speaking of the Church we mean the transmission (*paradosis*) of life.

As ye have therefore received Christ Jesus the Lord, so walk ye in him: rooted and built up in him, and stablished in the faith, as ye have been taught, abounding therein with thanksgiving. Beware lest any man spoil you through philosophy and vain deceit, after the tradition of men, after the rudiments of the world, and not after Christ (Col. 2: 6–8).

The Union of Church and Tradition

TRADITION and Church are not simply parallel concepts but realities which are essentially interrelated and bound together. Without being confounded they cannot be separated; they exist united together without confusion. Indeed, in a sense, the Church is Tradition, and Tradition, in its turn, is understood as the conscience of the Church. Hence, it is impossible for one to speak about Tradition without at the same time speaking about the Church. The teaching on Tradition is ecclesiology: indeed, the very heart of ecclesiology. Here Tradition is Christ, whom we have "received", as Saint Paul says; and it is precisely this Tradition that is the antithesis to the "tradition of men, after the rudiments of the world, and not after Christ".

When we say Tradition is Christ we mean that the Church refers back in Christ and through Christ to the sovereign principle of God the Father, to the source of Trinitarian and ecclesiastical unity: "There is one body, and one Spirit, even as ye are called in one hope of your calling; one Lord, one faith, one baptism, one God and Father of all, who is above all, and through all, and in you all" (Eph. 4:4–6). Thus we arrive at the source of the Church's unity, at the source of Tradition, at the cause of every gift.[2]

In the life of the supraessential and life-giving Trinity, the Father, who is the sole cause and principle of the hypostases,[3] gives himself over to the other two divine Persons, generating the Son and causing the Holy Spirit to proceed. We should understand this "giving over" (*paradosis*) as a communicating of all the divine essence of the Father to the Son and to the Holy Spirit, as a complete *kenôsis* of the Father. Primacy is here understood to be the extreme limit of love: the *paradosis* of the Father for the benefit of the other two persons. The Son and the Holy Spirit respond to this gushing forth of the Father's love. They do not *usurp* the Father's love for their own benefit, nor seize it (Phil. 2:6), but in their turn offer their existence and life – similarly, in love – to the Father. This exchange (*antidosis*) is expressed as absolute obedience to the Father's will.[4]

Similarly, in the Church, which is the image and reflection of the life of the triune God, the Son gives himself up for the life of the world (John 6:51). And here, too, there is an abundance of love and of offering. Here we have a giving over in love (*paradosis en agapê*). "For God so loved the word that he gave his only-begotten Son" (John 3:16). The Son's absolute obedience to the Father leads him to *kenôsis*, to humility, for the sake of the world's salvation. Likewise the Holy Spirit sojourned in the world to be a constant witness to the truth (John 15:26). Proceeding from the Father and being sent through the Son, the Holy Spirit, continues the work of Christ in history, being the Comforter of men.

The descent of the Holy Spirit, understood as *paradosis* and *enoikêsis* (indwelling) in the body of the Church, ensures the preservation of the truth and the new life. The Holy Spirit is given over (*paradidetai*) to the Church; it does not repeatedly descend upon the earth but abides and indwells in the historic Church. Pentecost is not an event belonging to the past: rather is it a continuous present in the life of the Church, a universal reality which embraces the Church and makes her a living image of eternity within the history of the world.

Thus, both within the relations between the three divine hypostases as well as within the Church (which in her turn is an image of the communion of the Trinity), God's love is manifested as *paradosis*, as a constant outpouring. God the Father gives himself over for the sake of the other two divine persons; the Son, out of love, becomes one of us and gives himself over to the race of men; finally, the Paraclete indwells the body of the Church until the *synteleia* of the ages and continues the Son's work in the world.

Revelation and Tradition

THE Holy Spirit's indwelling of the body of the Church means that the Church preserves the truth and revelation in the same way that a living body preserves its soul. Revelation – the culmination of which, as we know, is Pentecost – constitutes the primal factor in the life of the Church. The Church is alive because she possesses Revelation, and she possesses it precisely so that she can exist. In the final analysis, however, when we say that the Church possesses and preserves Revelation we mean to say that she does this because Revelation is Tradition (*paradosis*) and becomes Tradition within the Church. It is Tradition precisely because it was transmitted (*paradothê*) in Christ and in the Holy Spirit, and it becomes Tradition because the Church preserves it throughout the course of history, as the power of her life. In other words, Tradition is the unceasing existence of Revelation in the Church. It is that inner and cohesive power which holds the Church together. Through Tradition the Church is preserved alive and changeless simply because only in Tradition can the authentic message of Revelation be found, and only through Tradition does the life of the Church arrive at each given moment in time. From the very beginning of her existence up to the very present the Church is aware – with the same intensity now as then – of the presence of Christ and the Paraclete. Thus, the Church from the very first moment of her existence, to the very present, lives and experiences Revelation, and she shall continue to do so forever, since the gates of hell shall not prevail against her (Matt. 16:18). This living and reliving of Revelation in the Church, this continuous now of Revelation which is realized through Tradition, constitutes the very life of the Church: the gospel "which also we have received, and wherein we stand; by which also we are saved' (*cf.* 1 Cor. 15:1–2). Tradition, consequently, is the certainty that what we today possess is not something suspended in mid-air, but rather is organically connected with the life of Christ and with all that the apostles received. In other words, Tradition assures us of the eternity, inter-temporality and universality of the gospel, which is lived within the Church at each and every historical present, and which through the Church is conveyed to the world as the *kêrygma* of salvation.

Tradition and the Present Time

WE should at this point state that Tradition is not simply the voice of the past; it is rather the voice of eternity. Tradition is not a kind of sacred archaeology, nor even a reference to the experience of the past.

Tradition's value and significance is not to be found in that it is based upon an external historical authenticity, but in that it is based upon the unchanging and ever living voice of Revelation. This fidelity in Tradition does not simply mean a recognition of the historic past, but also an acceptance, in humility, of the word of God. Tradition is not only the testimony of history, the "yes" to the life of the past: rather, it is chiefly a reference to the truth which was revealed in Christ and is preserved in the Church in the Holy Spirit. Father Georges Florovsky puts it very well when he says:

> Tradition is not a principle striving to restore the past, using the past as a criterion for the present. Such a conception of tradition is rejected by history and by the consciousness of the Church. Tradition is *authority to teach, potestas magisterii, authority to bear witness to the truth.* The Church bears witness to the truth not by reminiscence or from the words of others, but from its own living, unceasing experience, from its catholic fulness . . . Therein consists that 'tradition of truth', *traditio veritatis,* about which St Irenaeus spoke. For him it is connected with the 'veritable unction of truth', *charisma veritatis certum,* and the 'teaching of the Apostles' was for him not so much an unchangeable example to be repeated or imitated, as an eternally living and inexhaustible source of life and inspiration. Tradition is the constant abiding of the Spirit and not only the memory of words. Tradition is a *charismatic,* not a historical, principle.[5]

Tradition, as a charismatic event, as an unceasing revelation of the word of God in the Holy Spirit at each specific historical present, is not something distant, something springing from history and which one must discover by going centuries back, but it is a reality which is extremely contemporary, just as the fruits of the Spirit ("love, joy, peace, longsuffering, gentleness, goodness, faith, meekness, temperance" [Gal. 5:22–23]) are extremely contemporary for the life of modern man. Tradition is ever present, here and now. It is always open, ready to embrace the present and accept the future. Just as the Church at every given historical moment accepts new members, so too is Tradition tangible and believable in every age, simply because the Church is the living bearer of Tradition.

The contemporaneity of Tradition is based on the unbroken presence of Christ in the Church, and on the certainty that the teacher of the Church is the Holy Spirit. Patriarch Dositheus of Jerusalem in his Confession (1672) writes:

We believe the catholic Church to be taught by the Holy Spirit. For he is the true Paraclete, whom Christ sends from the Father in order to teach the truth and to dispel the darkness from the minds of the faithful. The teaching [*didachê*] of the Holy Spirit, however, does not directly make the Church splendid and brilliant, but indirectly, through the fathers and leaders of the catholic Church.[6]

The denial of Tradition's importance is essentially the denial of the work of the Holy Spirit in history and the doubting of his *charismata*. In the final analysis, to reject Tradition means to reject the Church as the body of Christ and as the vessel of the Holy Spirit. By calling into question the fact that Tradition possesses tremendous importance for the here and now of the Church, if we deny that Tradition is the image of the catholic and inter-temporal nature of the Church, we reduce and alter the Church from its "God-Manness" to a simple society of men, based exclusively on human standards. Rejecting Tradition is like accepting that Christ has forsaken the Church, that his words, "and, lo, I am with you always, even unto the end of the world" (Matt. 28:20), and "I will pray the Father, and he shall give you another Comforter, that he may abide with you for ever" (John 14:16), are in the end a deception. By accepting the premise that we today are able to understand and to interpret the gospel by basing ourselves solely on our brilliance and experience, without Tradition, we strip the Church naked of Christ; we sever the body from the head, we take away its life-giving Spirit, thus leaving the gospel open to individual judgement and to the arbitrary whims of our own subjectivity. The Orthodox Patriarchs of the East in their famous Encyclical of 1848 describe very simply and yet with complete theological fullness this living continuity of Tradition:

For our faith, brethren, is neither from men nor by man, but by the revelation of Jesus Christ, which the holy apostles preached, the sacred ecumenical councils upheld, the most great and wise doctors of the *oikoumene* transmitted through their teaching, and the holy martyrs confirmed with their blood. We hold pure the confession which we have received.[7]

We cannot deny the life of the Church, that "unbroken chain", which defines the "sacred enclosure" of the Church, "the door of which is Christ and in which the entire Orthodox fold is shepherded".[8]

Tradition and the People of God

THE question is thus posed: How can we test the genuineness of
Tradition? The Patriarchs of the East give the following answer in
their Encyclical: "The defender of the faith is the body of the Church,
that is the people [*laos*]."⁹ The people of God, taken together as a
whole, possesses a spiritual sense with which it can test whether or
not, and to what extent, our actions and *kêrygmata* are in accordance with the life and word of the catholic Church. Thus Tradition
is protected within the entire ecclesiastical body. The hierarchy of
the Church teaches, that is, it interprets Tradition, and the *laos*
in its entirety makes declarations concerning its faithfulness to
Tradition. Here we have an inner reciprocity. The teachers of the
Church interpret Tradition, they transmit the gospel to the people,
and the *laos* judges whether or not the interpretation transmitted
to it is authentic or not. This means that all who interpret the gospel
can never disregard the people, because the *laos* in its entirety is the
bearer of Tradition. Thus it is that both those who teach and those
who are taught, both hierarchy and people, constitute a whole
which labours for the preservation of the truth, for the protection
and understanding of Tradition. Each from his own viewpoint
contributes to the same task. The hierarchy passes judgement on
tradition, and the *laos* judges the judgements of the hierarchy. Thus
it endorses its teaching and its decisions. When Saint Paul wrote
to the Thessalonians, "hold the traditions" (2 Thess. 2:15), he
was acknowledging precisely this: the right which the *laos* has
to maintain the Tradition and to reject every foreign element
which might affect the purity of the life of the Church.

Thus it is that the entire body of the faithful carries out a
tremendous task in preserving the genuineness of Tradition. With
the instinct which comes from the very experience of Tradition
itself it is able to ascertain what is contained in the *consensus
patrum et apostolorum* and what remains outside of it. This special
sense which the people of God possesses and which in the end makes
the people the "guardian of the faith" is nothing other than the fruit
of the very same experience lived by the apostles and received and
lived by the fathers and the saints of the Church and preserved alive

in every historical present of the Church. Thus, it is the identity of the experience which ensures the faithfulness of Tradition. Throughout the ages the Church preaches and lives the very same gospel, the very same truth. And of course this truth is not an idea, a concept, but a specific person, the *theandric* person of Christ (John 14:6). Christ then is "the same yesterday, and today, and for ever" (Heb. 13:8), and the Holy Spirit vivifies the faithful and ensures the unity of life. Thus, the experience of the faithful people of God today is not of another order than the experiences of the saints and the apostles. And it is this one and the same experience of the people of God which in the final analysis is fidelity to Tradition.

It is should be understood that when we speak about fidelity to Tradition we do not deprive the Church of the right, nor do we call into question her obligation, to express in a new way, relevant to the needs of each and every age, the one unique gospel message. On the contrary, fidelity to Tradition very often compels us to abandon the forms and *schemata* of the past. Thus, fidelity to Tradition never hindered the fathers of the Church in expressing in new terminology and in a new fashion all that the Church had already lived and experienced from the very beginning of her existence. Hence, whatever the fathers or ecumenical councils stated in later times, precisely because it sprang from the same catholic fullness, is of equal value and authenticity with whatever was said from the very beginning.

Tradition and traditions

AT this point it is necessary to recall the difference between Tradition and traditions. What we have written thus far has had this distinction in mind. The tradition of men should not be confused with the catholic fullness of the life of the Church, with the one universal Tradition. In contrast to this one Tradition, which constitutes the conscience and the identity of the Church throughout the ages, traditions are the work of human hands; they come and go, change and are supplemented, are rejected or sustained, depending upon the prevailing spiritual climate. These traditions may be useful, positive, and creative, but they can also be without meaning, or even the result of man's sinfulness. They may possibly help in the understanding of

Tradition, but then again, they may also become an insurmountable
obstacle in approaching the Christian message.

Therefore, when we speak about Tradition, we do not mean
all those human elements which are encountered in the historical
Church, but the one and only deposit of faith which is found in the
Church, and because of which the Church is "the pillar and ground of
the truth" (1 Tim. 3:15). The Joint Doctrinal Commission appointed
by the Ecumenical Patriarch and the Archbishop of Canterbury for
consultation on the points of agreement and difference between
the Anglican and the Eastern Orthodox Churches (1930) issued the
following statement:

We agree that by Holy Tradition we mean the truths which came
down from our Lord and the Apostles through the Fathers, which are
confessed unanimously and continuously in the Undivided Church,
and are taught by the Church under the guidance of the Holy Spirit.

Everything necessary for salvation can be founded upon Holy Scripture
as completed, explained, interpreted, and understood in the Holy
Tradition, by the guidance of the Holy Spirit residing in the Church.

We agree that nothing contained in Tradition is contrary to the Scriptures. Though these two may be logically defined and distinguished,
yet they cannot be separated from each other nor from the Church.

Scripture and Tradition

It is now necessary that we briefly examine here the question of
Scripture and Tradition. Generally speaking, Scripture and Tradition
should neither be separated nor confused ("though these two may
be logically defined and distinguished yet they cannot be separated
from each other nor from the Church"). Scripture and Tradition
constitute an unbroken whole, the one is contained within the other.
Or if we wish to be more explicit, Scripture is contained within
Tradition. Paul put it quite clearly in Thessalonians: "brethren, stand
fast, and hold the traditions which ye have been taught, whether by
word, or our epistle" (2 Thess. 2:15). Tradition is channelled into the
Church through word and through the Scripture. Here there is no
relationship either of superiority or subordination. The spoken
word and Scripture possess a mutuality and agreement, a mutual

fulfilment and confirmation. As Saint Basil puts it, "both have equal force for piety".[11] And Saint John Chrysostom was to add, "they did not transmit all things through epistles; much was handed over not in writing. In like manner, both these and those are worthy of belief. Hence, we consider the Tradition of the Church also worthy of belief. Is it Tradition? Then inquire no more".[12]

In Western Christianity the distinction between Scripture and Tradition was more firmly stressed. Thus they are either considered as "two sources of Revelation" (Rome) or else Tradition is completely rejected so as to create the concept of *sola scriptura* (the Reformation). Actually, there is no difference between Rome and the Reformation in this regard. In both instances the distinction between Scripture and Tradition is emphasized. Rome views Scripture and Tradition as two sources of the faith, while the Reformers opt for Scripture alone. In both cases the belief that Scripture and Tradition are two different things is presupposed.

Against such a viewpoint, which in the end reduces the spiritual relationship between Scripture and Tradition to a legalistic one (of equality or superiority), the East posits her own understanding of the matter, which is based on the principle that Scripture and Tradition coexist within the Church. The Church, guided by the Holy Spirit, understands Scripture (composed with the inspiration of the Holy Spirit) in the light of Tradition (also the work of the Holy Spirit).

Church, Scripture and Tradition

IN other words, Tradition is Scripture interpreted by the Church. And just as the Church understands Scripture in the light of Tradition, so in like manner does she understand Tradition in the light of Scripture. Tradition is full of Scripture; that is why her theology, the theology of the fathers and the councils, is nothing other than biblical theology.

Scripture and Tradition are mutually understood and exist together. Both are united unshakeably with the Church. Scripture is born in the Church and for the Church, and Tradition bears from the very beginning the seal of the Church. It is in the Church that Scripture and Tradition appear and are contained. Thus

Scripture, Tradition and the Church are linked through an inner relationship, a harmonious co-existence, a mutual supplementation and agreement. Scripture and Tradition as revelationary-charismatic realities are contained within the Church which is also a revelationary-charismatic reality.

Those who separate Holy Scripture, Tradition and the Church come to the false conclusion that either Scripture is superior to the Church and Tradition, or that the Church is superior to Scripture. The first opinion is to be found among Protestant theologians, the latter in Roman Catholic theology. This hyperbole leads to an alteration of the meaning of the Church, either to an under-evaluation (subordination) or to an over-evaluation. By placing the Bible over and above the Church and Tradition we destroy the balance, we corrupt its' canonical position, and take the first step towards an individualistic theology outside the Church. On the other hand, the idea that the Church is superior to Holy Scripture leads to the opinion that the Church is able to elicit every dogma from within herself. Only if we accept that the Church, Tradition and Scripture are neither separated nor confused, being united without confusion, will we be able to understand that the Church alone is she who can find the true meaning of Holy Scripture, just as the Son alone is he who is able to understand the words of the Father.

NOTES

* A paper given at the Anglican–Orthodox Joint Discussions held at Chambésy in July 1981, and first published in *Sobornost* 4 (1982), 30–37.

1. Gregory of Nyssa, *On the Song of Songs,* ed. H. Langerbeck, pp. 384, 386; PG 44:1049BC, 1052A.

2. "For every good gift is from above and comes down from Thee, the Father of lights . . . ", *The Divine Liturgy of Saint John Chrysostom.*

3. M. Farantos, "Orthodoxy and Contemporary Reality", *Koinonia* (1977), 32.

4. *Ibid.*

5. G. Florovsky, "Sobornost: The Catholicity of the Church", in *The Church of God: An Anglo–Russian Symposium,* ed. E. L. Mascall (London, 1934), pp. 64–65.

6. J. N. Karmiris, *The Dogmatic and Symbolic Monuments of the Orthodox Catholic Church* ii (Graz, 1968), p. 835.

7. *Ibid.,* p. 1002.

8. *Ibid.,* p. 1003.

9. *Ibid.,* p. 1000.

10. *Lambeth Occasional Reports 1931–1938* (London, 1948), pp. 52–53.

11. *On the Holy Spirit,* PG 32:188A ff.

12. *Homily 4, 2 on 2 Thessalonians,* ed. B. de Montfaucon, Vol. 11, in *Ioannis Chrysostomi opera omnia quae extant vel eius nomine circumferuntur* (Paris, 1718–1738), 532B.

13. C. Scouteris, "Holy Scripture and Councils", *Sobornost* 7, 2 (1975), pp. 112–113 [reprinted in the present edition]. See also D. Staniloae, "Holy Scripture in relation to the Church and Tradition", *The Living Logos: A Spiritual Symposium on Holy Scripture* (Athens, 1970), p. 83.

The Ecclesiastical Significance of the WCC

THE FUSION OF DOCTRINE AND LIFE*

I

WHEN ONE SPEAKS OF THE ECCLESIASTICAL significance of the World Council of Churches (WCC) one often risks several dangers. This is because within the family of churches which constitute the World Council of Churches there are various ecclesiological positions differing from one another in theological principles and presuppositions. Furthermore, it is now commonly admitted that for all churches, even more for the World Council of Churches, it has become increasingly difficult to speak with a single voice.[1] The World Council, being a large communion of churches, naturally allows, and in many cases encourages, the expression of a variety of opinions according to specific circumstances. Thus one and the same person may be found stressing one ecclesiological aspect in one context, and in another a different one.

Having accepted this ecclesiological pluralism as the *modus operandi* within the World Council, let us endeavour to distinguish the main factors which characterize the World Council of Churches and which manifest the ecclesiastical significance of this living body. This certainly does not mean that our intent here is to list historical events or decisions, but rather to go beyond them and to discover their message and their significance both for the Council and for the member churches. In other words, my aim in this article is not to show the historical development of the ecumenical commitment of the member churches but to reflect, somewhat critically, from my own personal observation, on how this commitment has manifested itself at various stages since Amsterdam. What we seek is not to dwell in detail on the events but to find out what is the moving force behind these events.

II

In this perspective we first have to consider theologically the very fact of the creation of the World Council of Churches. The question is, what did Amsterdam represent for the future of the Council as well as for the churches themselves? We may look at the question from another standpoint. Was the significance of Amsterdam limited only to the fact that a fellowship of churches was created? It seems to me that, although the existence of this fellowship is of capital importance, it is not the only message of Amsterdam. Let me clarify. It is clear that the Amsterdam Assembly marked the formal establishment of the World Council of Churches. The new organization arose out of the coming together of two earlier movements, Faith and Order, and Life and Work. These two movements as multi-church organizations had previously acted separately, each with its own objectives and its own theological orientation. Faith and Order had dealt more specifically with matters of a theological and ecclesiological nature. Its main interest was to clarify questions of faith, to discern the common doctrinal inheritance of the churches as well as to acknowledge sincerely their doctrinal differences. The movement also devoted itself to the study of matters of church order, that is, to the study of questions related to the nature of the Church as a visible community, the ministry of the Church, and the sacraments of the Church. On the other hand, the Life and Work movement sought to implement the Christian faith in the life and activity of people. Its concern was to deal with practical matters confronting the churches and the society: moral and racial problems, social and international relationships, questions of unemployment, economic crises, education, and so forth.

The amalgamation of the two movements to form the World Council of Churches concealed, I believe, a desire to discover and a process to reach what we may call a common Christian ethos. I speak not of an external collaboration or of an "agreement", in the sense most commonly used, but of a common commitment to follow creatively what may be characterized as and corresponds to the "Christian way". The union of Faith and Order and of Life and Work was certainly a commitment to a new orientation,[2] but it also revealed the sincere desire of Christians to move towards a more catholic and apostolic understanding of their response to the call of God and *of their work*. This dramatic shift of emphasis was, to a great extent, unconscious. The fact that the two differently-oriented movements desired to come together suggests that the pioneers of the ecumenical movement had started to question the theological quality, the validity and the genuineness of their work thus far. It also suggests that they realized, although perhaps not fully, that to draw a sharp distinction between doctrine and the daily life and work of people is not only "academic", but also involves a distortion of the very nature of the Christian message.

It is essential for our investigation to give special attention to the fact that throughout Christian history the Church has suffered from the pressure of two opposing tendencies; or, if you will, it was often faced by a double dilemma. The church was always tempted either to follow the path of institutionalism, leading to an over-emphasis on Christian action, to a Christian activism, so to speak, or that of a spiritualistic approach, leading to a monistic understanding of the Christian teaching. The charge of institutionalism is often brought up against Roman Catholicism, while that of spiritualism against Protestantism; but I believe this to be a very serious over-simplification.[3] The point is that these tendencies have always existed in Christian communities in one form or another as a temptation, and that each one of them has shown to a greater or lesser extent the same failure, that is, to give due place to the truth that the Christian message and the Christian way cannot be divided into "faith" and "work".

Perhaps the most lasting contribution of Amsterdam to the churches was this very fact of the merging of the two movements in order to create a new fellowship. This delineated the physiognomy of the Council. At the same time, it was an example for and a challenge to the churches to realize that their task is first to understand and then to preach the gospel as a unique and catholic reality which covers and illuminates every aspect of human life. By saying this, I do not wish to create the impression that I am unaware of difficulties or that today the danger of falling into one or the other of the above temptations is absent from the life and activity of the Council. I simply wish to underline the fact that the vocation which the World Council of Churches has undertaken is to remind itself first and then its member churches that a sharp distinction between doctrine and life leads to a distortion of the Christian message.

If we examine the apostolic teaching and the patristic under-standing of this teaching, we will see that the unity between doctrine and practical Christian work is the necessary presupposition for the fulfilment of Christ's commission, that is, the mission of the Church. This means that the concern for the practical implications of the gospel and for the theological work are not two different tasks but they coexist in the Church and both are equally connected with what is called by the fathers "pastoral pathos".[4]

It is not surprising, therefore, to observe that the ecclesiastical significance of the World Council is intimately related to the very origin of this new body which had committed itself from its inception to see Christian life in its wholeness. It means that the establishment of this "new phenomenon" in ecclesiastical history does not simply manifest the desire for *rapprochement* but also indicates its determination to see and to serve the Christian gospel in its integral and catholic dimension.

III

THIS in no way means that the Council is a "Super Church". It has repeatedly been said that the World Council of Churches "is not a new church (even less a Super Church) and does not perform ecclesiastical functions".[5] This was clearly set forth at the very moment of the Council's formation. In the Constitution it is said that: "The World Council shall not legislate for the churches", while in the official explanatory memorandum it is stated that the Assembly and the Central Committee "will have no constitutional authority whatever over its constituent churches".[6] Thus the Council arose as an absolutely new phenomenon, a fellowship of churches. This fellowship has its own unique character and is without precedent in ecclesiastical history; it has its own specific source and its own unique and characteristic task. In fact, the creation of the World Council of Churches is the realization of hopes and dreams which had been previously expressed by many people of widely differing ecclesiastical backgrounds and traditions. The famous "Encyclical Letter" of the Ecumenical Patriarch in 1920 proposed the creation of a *koinonia* of the churches. A year earlier, in 1919, Archbishop Söderblom had written: "What I advocate is an Ecumenical Council of Churches. This should not be given external authority but would make its influence felt in so far as it can act with spiritual authority. It would not speak *ex cathedra*, but from the depth of the Christian conscience."

The conception of a "fellowship of churches" introduced by the founders of the World Council of Churches to describe the new organism should be more carefully examined. The scriptural word which corresponds most closely to the idea of such a fellowship is the Greek *koinonia*. In the New Testament it means "to share something in common". Obviously the nature of this common sharing is determined by that in which the participants are involved. Thus in the New Testament we see basically two forms of sharing: (1) sharing on a material level (Rom. 15:26; 2 Cor. 9:13; Heb. 13:16), and (2) sharing on a level which transcends the material interests of people and therefore cannot be adequately expressed in intellectual terms. This latter form of sharing surpasses empirical experience and is a divine-human communion. In the New Testament it is described as a communion with God the Father, Christ, or the Holy Spirit (1 Cor. 1:9; 2 Cor. 13:14; Phil. 3:10; 1 John 1:3, 6). This divine-human communion appears as an ecclesial fellowship (Acts 2:42; Phil. 1:5; 2:1–2; 1 John 1:7, and so on).

It has its inward quality in what is termed a "mystery of gathering-together". In other words, the ecclesial fellowship is based and expressed in the eucharist. "The cup of blessing which we bless, is it not the communion of the blood of Christ? The bread which we break, is it not the communion of the body of Christ? For we being many are one bread, and one body: for we are all partakers of that one bread" (1 Cor. 10:16–17). Thus it is essential to note that, in the mind of the apostolic church, the eucharist, ecclesial body and fellowship, constitute a divine-human interpenetration.

Such an understanding of fellowship is a recurring theme throughout Christian history and more clearly in patristic thought. It is not difficult to present patristic citations, but I offer by way of summary just one passage from the works of Nicholas Cabasilas (fourteenth century):

The whole Church is called holy, and the apostle, writing to the Christian people as a whole, says to them: "Holy brethren, partakers of the heavenly calling" (Heb. 3:1). The faithful are called saints because of the Holy Thing of which they partake, because of Him Whose Body and Blood they receive. Members of His Body, flesh of His Flesh and bone of His Bone, as long as we remain united to Him and preserve our connection with Him, we live by holiness, drawing to ourselves, through the Holy Mysteries, the sanctity which comes from that Head and that Heart. But if we should cut ourselves off, if we should separate ourselves from the unity of this most holy Body, we partake of the Holy Mysteries in vain, for life cannot flow into dead and amputated limbs.[7]

Further, it must be stated that this biblical-patristic understanding of the term fellowship in no way suggests a collective reality which stands over human persons. It is certainly not something controlling human persons from outside or dominating them from above. Fellowship requires absolute respect for the human personality; it always presupposes the free choice of the human person. Nicholas Berdyaev draws a very clear distinction between fellowship and collectivism.

There is an absolute difference between the life of community on the one hand and collectivism on the other. The former is the brotherly communion in truth on the part of human beings whose freedom is an accepted fact. Collectivism on the other hand is a compulsory organization of the community; it is the recognition of the collective as a special kind of reality which stands above human personality and oppresses it by its authority.[8]

Lastly, this full ecclesial, that is eucharistic, fellowship should never be viewed as a static condition, but rather as a continuous dynamic process. Although the eucharist is the "fullness", at the same time it is an opening for a personal growth from "glory to glory". In the patristic tradition, life within the Church is never understood as a *stasis* or as an end. It is quite false to confine ecclesial life within the narrow bounds of an established historical institution. The church which, from its own being and its own life, bears witness to the fullness of the Christian gospel, offers immense potentialities to each believer to create his or her own personal history of salvation. This personal history is a continuous progress within the Church towards the unending end of perfection. Thus the life of the Church as a life of communion of the human being with God and also with one's fellow beings is not confined within limits, but indeed is an infinite life; it is offered to each believer by the Holy Spirit as a possibility "to comprehend with all the saints what is the breadth, and length, and depth, and height; And to know the love of Christ, which passeth knowledge, that ye might be filled with all the fulness of God" (Eph. 3:18–19). "What we have already received of the blessed nature of the Good at every moment is great", says Saint Gregory of Nyssa, "but that which lies beyond our grasp is always infinitely greater."[9]

As we have already pointed out, when the World Council of Churches was established in 1948, its founders adopted the word fellowship to designate the new body. The World Council of Churches has been described as "a fellowship of churches which accept our Lord as God and Saviour". But soon after its formation, questions began to arise from different ecclesiastical circles concerning the ecclesial status of the newly created Council. For a number of years thereafter great attention was given by many involved in the ecumenical commitment to defining the ecclesiological significance of the World Council of Churches. The crucial question was whether this fellowship of churches should be considered an ecclesial reality. In the final analysis, what is the nature of the fellowship of the World Council of Churches? It was essential that the member churches reach a clear understanding of the nature of their fellowship within the new organization so as to be sure of their position and responsibilities.

The questions were certainly approached with a sense of great responsibility and urgency. The result of this search was the production of a statement, adopted by the Central Committee at Toronto in 1950, on "The Church, the Churches and the World Council of Churches".[10]

This statement attempted to clarify what the World Council of Churches was and what it was not.[11] One can see this as a response to fears, misunderstandings and questions raised about the nature and function of the Council. It was essential that light be thrown on the phenomenon of this fellowship of the churches, given that such a fellowship had no precedent. I think one is justified in calling attention to the Toronto statement for basically two reasons: (1) it clearly defined the relation of the member churches to one another within the fellowship; (2) it created a theological framework within which a deeper understanding of such a "fellowship of churches" could be explored.

In light of Toronto's clarifications it is clear that the World Council of Churches is *not* a new, autonomous ecclesiastical establishment with its own credal basis. It is, rather, a fellowship in which the churches come to know each other. The basis for this coming together of the churches is their common desire to witness to the divinity and saving work of Jesus Christ. After a long period during which the various Christian communities had ignored one another, through this Council they entered into a serious commitment to approach and to understand one another. Within this fellowship they had committed themselves to strive mutually to share experiences, to study in common their theological agreements and differences, and to present a common and faithful witness to the lordship of Christ in the world. In other words, the fellowship of which we speak has its own peculiar vocation. As had already been pointed out at Amsterdam, it is "an event without precedent in the history of the Church".[12]

The significance and the character of the World Council of Churches as a fellowship of churches, its intention and its basis, were reaffirmed in a statement produced by the Second Assembly at Evanston. Among other things that statement says:

The World Council of Churches is an instrument at the service of the churches which enables them to enter into fraternal conversation with

each other, to cooperate in various fields, and to render witness together
to the world . . . Since the Council desires to make clear to the churches
and to the world what it is, what it does, and who are its members, it has
adopted a basis . . . This basis performs three functions: (1) It indicates
the nature of the fellowship which the churches in the Council seek to
establish among themselves. For that fellowship, as a fellowship of churches,
has its own unique character. It has a specific source and a specific dynamic.
The churches enter into relation with each other because there is a unity
given once for all in the person and work of their common Lord and because
the Living Lord gathers His people together. (2) It provides the orientation
point for the work which the World Council undertakes. The ecumenical
conversations which take place in the World Council must have a point
of reference. Similarly, the activities of the Council must be submitted
to an ultimate norm and standard. The basis provides that standard. (3) It
indicates the range of the fellowship which the churches seek to establish.

From these and similar declarations it is clear that this fellowship
of churches within the World Council is not, strictly speaking, a
communion in the biblical-patristic sense, that is, in eucharistic
fullness. It is rather a fellowship "in progress": a fellowship calling
the churches towards the goal of full eucharistic communion.
Within this unique body, the churches are called and seek to express
through their common work and their common witness their already
existing unity, while at the same time undertaking the urgent vocation
to prepare the way for an ever deeper understanding of that unity and
for a fuller coming together. It is against this background that we
must consider the expansion of the original Christological position
which had been set forth in its Constitution as the basis for the
Council's existence into a Trinitarian one. The Trinitarian formulation encompasses a broader range of the Christian belief. It is not a
clarification or amplification of an abstract doctrinal formulation
but a further step towards a fuller and more stable fellowship,[13] in so
far as throughout the entire Christian tradition the one God in Trinity
has always been considered as the *Alpha* and the *Omega* of the life of the
Church. It is from the Trinitarian God that the life of the Church springs.

IV

THE Council's role has always been understood as that of preparation and facilitation. The Council has from the beginning of its
existence sought to serve the churches as an instrument, to lighten

their task and their way towards the one eucharistic fellowship. Its initial vocation was to transform the indifference to the need for ecumenical fellowship and unity into a deep, conscious conviction that Christianity itself, in its very essence, is unity. Isolation and disunity are anomalies which can only be understood as the result of sin and evil. It is interesting to note that in patristic thought sin and evil have, in general, been described as decomposition, disorganization, and a dissolution of the unity created by God. This disunity, as a disrupted condition, leads to selfishness and to a sectarian, monistic understanding of the Christian gospel.[14] In this perspective the task to promote unity is not always an easy one, given that our societies are pluralistic and, as such, easily accept or encourage diversity. Thus, often theological justifications of diversity are welcomed, while in many cases the need for unity is under-stressed. The way towards unity is, unfortunately, often considered to be an illusion or as a religious Utopia or, in some cases, as something not of first importance or, even worse, as something unnecessary. Many supporting arguments are brought forward, as for example the often expressed position that in the New Testament one cannot find a single ecclesiology, or that one can find therein more support for diversity than for unity, and so on.[15]

I think that one of the most important and comprehensive declarations of the Council in connection with this commitment to serve the churches on their way towards union was that adopted by the Assembly in Nairobi (1975). This declaration, the result of work extending over many years, is included in the Council's Constitution and describes its function in a positive way. According to this affirmation, the World Council has the vocation "to call the churches to the goal of the visible unity in one faith and one eucharistic fellowship expressed in worship and in common life in Christ, and to advance towards that unity in order that the world may believe".

The essence of the desired unity is here defined as a unity "in one faith and one eucharistic fellowship". This means that unity in its eucharistic fullness, this ultimate goal of every serious ecumenical attempt, should be reduced neither to the level of sentimentality nor that of "academic" discussions, but presupposes and is achieved through "the common faith". Such full unity is to be realized through the unifying action of the Holy Spirit, and must be based on the rock of "the common confession of faith". In other words, common faith is the *sine qua non* of the visible unity. This implies a return to the common ground of the apostolic faith, that faith which "is neither from man nor by man, but by the revelation of Jesus Christ, which the holy apostles preached, the sacred Ecumenical Councils upheld, the most great and wise doctors of the *oecumene* transmitted through their teaching, and the holy martyrs confirmed with their blood".[16]

It has been said in many ways that the fundamental vocation of the World Council of Churches is to serve the divided and separated churches. At the risk of repetition, it must again be reaffirmed that the Council is neither a new ecclesial establishment nor a part of the "ecclesiastical machinery"[17] in general, but rather, both a challenging and facilitating organ. According to the Toronto Declaration, the purpose of the World Council is "to bring the churches into contact with one another and to promote discussion of questions of Church unity". It may be helpful to focus our attention on the two basic levels of service by which the Council enables the churches to enter into fraternal relations.

a) *Common theological work:* When we speak of common theological work, we designate both that work done within the Council on its own initiative and with the participation of various people from various churches, as well as that work done outside the Council but through its mediation. As examples of the first case, one can cite the work of various international consultations within the Faith and Order Commission leading to an agreement on baptism, eucharist and ministry as well as the project "Towards the Common Expression of the Apostolic Faith Today", an attempt to move towards a deeper understanding and explication of the apostolic faith as it has been expressed in the Nicene-Constantinopolitan Creed (325 and 381). In the second case, one can note the mediation of the World Council and the assistance rendered by it in order to make possible the fruitful theological discussions between the Orthodox churches and the Oriental Orthodox churches. It must be stressed here that it became increasingly apparent during the history of the World

Council of Churches that the churches, in order to achieve a fuller mutual fellowship, must honestly confront their differing convictions. They also have the spiritual responsibility to confess afresh the one apostolic faith. The declaration of the Vancouver Assembly is very significant: the churches are called "to share a common understanding of the apostolic faith, and be able to confess this message together in ways understandable, reconciling and liberating".

b) *Cooperation at the practical level:* The ministerial role of the Council is certainly not, and cannot be limited to, theological collaboration. Likewise, the Council is called to serve the churches to the best of its ability as an instrument facilitating their commitment to cooperate on various practical levels. This cooperation not only includes help to cover crucial human situations throughout the world but also an initiative and common advocacy of the member churches in regard to questions of freedom and justice, social problems, oppression, and so forth. This common work is evidently based on the mandate to love our neighbour and to consider him or her as a member of the one body of the human race in which we all share: "And whether one member suffer, all the members suffer with it" (1 Cor. 12:26). It must be said here that this task of cooperation is not always an easy one when one takes into account the differing socio-economic conditions in which the churches find themselves. One certainly cannot ignore the considerable work done in this area during the forty-year history of the Council, and that this work has drawn the different churches closer to one another.

This function of the World Council of Churches is, to a great extent, fulfilled through participation, communication, and generally through maintaining contacts in various ways. In other words, the task of the Council during the forty years of its history was and still is to promote such cooperation between the churches, to be a *locus* and means of their *rapprochement*. Its very existence is based on the principle of participation. This means that the opinions of the member churches are of capital importance when decisions and initiatives are undertaken. We must stress that the function of representative cooperation works both ways: the representatives are the voices of their churches within and to the Council, but also the voice of the Council to their respective churches. In order to promote closer contacts, it was absolutely necessary for the Council to generate an atmosphere of confidence and understanding. *Rapprochement* could only be realizable and effective through humility and absolute respect for the member churches. This was clearly expressed in the statement of the Central Committee in 1972: "We shall have to learn to be better and more humble listeners to one another. Listening is especially needed where the fellowship is rent apart by human tensions and where men can only affirm it in darkness."[18]

NOTES

*This paper was first published in *The Ecumenical Review,* Vol. 40, nos. 3–4. *Commemorating Amsterdam 1948: 40 Years of the World Council of Churches* (Geneva, 1988), 519–527.

1. D. J. Johnson, ed., *Uppsala to Nairobi* (New York and London, 1975), p. 28.

2. What is said in the Amsterdam Message is very significant: "Here at Amsterdam, we have committed ourselves afresh to Him and have covenanted with one another in constituting this World Council of Churches. We intend to stay together."

3. N. A. Matsoukas, *The Ecumenical Movement* (Thessalonica, 1986), p. 249 [in Greek].

4. Saint Gregory of Nyssa, *On the Day of Lights in the which Our Lord was Baptized,* ed. E. Gebhardt, p. 221, 12; PG. 46:577A.

5. Statement of the Evanston Assembly, 1954. For further discussion of this issue, see W. A. Visser 't Hooft, "Super-Church and the Ecumenical Movement", *The Ecumenical Review* 10, no. 4 (1957–1958), 365 ff.

6. See Visser 't Hooft, "The Significance of the World Council of Churches", in *The Universal Church in God's Design,* p. 181. Quoted by T. Sartory, *The Oecumenical Movement and the Unity of the Church* (Oxford, 1963), pp. 22–23.

7. *A Commentary on the Divine Liturgy* 36, trans. G. M. Hussey and P. A. McNulty (London, 1966), p. 89. Capitalization mine.

8. *Truth and Revelation* (London, 1953), p. 25.

9. *On the Song of Songs* 8, ed. H. Langerbeck, pp. 245, 23–2462; PG 44:940D–941A.

10. *The Ecumenical Review* 3 (1950), 47–53.

11. *Uppsala to Nairobi, op. cit.,* p. 23. See also *The Ecumenical Advance: A History of the Ecumenical Movement,* Vol. 2 (1948–1968), ed. H. E. Fey (Geneva, 1986), pp. 29–30.

12. Visser 't Hooft, *The First Assembly of the World Council of Churches: Man's Disorder and God's Design,* Vol. 5 (London, 1949), p. 28, quoted in T. Sartory, *op. cit,* p. 25.

13. For the history and for a further discussion of the basis of the WCC, see H. Krüger, "The Life and Activities of the World Council of Churches", *The Ecumenical Advance, op. cit.,* pp. 33 ff.

14. See my article, "The People of God – its Unity and its Glory: a Discussion of John 17:17–24 in the Light of Patristic Thought", *The Greek Orthodox Theological Review* 30 (1985), 409 ff [reprinted in the present edition].

15. L. Vischer, " . . . If Time Permits. Report on Church Union", *The Ecumenical Review* 23 (1971), 144.

16. *Encyclical of the Orthodox Patriarchs of the East of 1848.*

17. Visser 't Hooft, *Has the Ecumenical Movement a Future?* (Belfast, 1974), p. 40.

18. Quoted in *Uppsala to Nairobi, op. cit.,* p. 28.

Common Prayer*

THE QUESTION OF JOINT PRAYER has been a recurrent topic in ecumenical meetings and theological dialogues. The reasons why this subject has remained ecumenically apposite, and why it has occupied the Orthodox world, are many, because of the relevance of this topic to theology, history and the canonical tradition of the Orthodox Church. We must note together with this that from the beginning Orthodox theologians have presented distinct understandings of the question of joint prayer, depending to a large degree on their theological concerns, their interpretation of history, and the canonical tradition.

The Unity of Theology and Prayer

IN theology, and in the life of the Orthodox Church, there has always existed an inseparable connection between dogma and worship, between theology and prayer. Orthodox prayer and worship did not constitute a "chapter" independent from the faith of the Church, rather it was a devotional-liturgical expression of the one and inseparable dogmatic teaching of the Church. The *lex orandi* [*est*] *lex credendi* has always been an inviolable canon which defined the Orthodox ethos. This approach is clearly expressed by the words of Evagrius: "If you are a theologian, you will pray in truth; and if you pray in truth, you are a theologian."[1]

It should be stressed that the term "Orthodoxy" does not merely indicate right opinion or belief as opposed to heresy, but also right *glorification*. More accurately, it indicates right glorification as something which encompasses right belief, and a right way of expressing belief. Thus, right doxology – or simply doxology – is a more comprehensive definition than right belief.

We must make it clear that, according to an Orthodox understanding, doctrinal tradition is not exclusively an intellectual exercise or a system of thought. Rather, it is inextricably bound together with liturgical action. It is within the worshipping community, and in light of the community's liturgical life, that doctrine becomes "a field of vision wherein all things on earth are seen in their relation to the things of heaven".[2] In this respect, the *lex orandi* becomes the focus of the *lex credendi*, of the *lex cognoscendi,* and of the *lex vivendi:* in other words, the dogmas are not abstract speculations in and of themselves. Likewise, the Christian life is not a moralistic and external behaviour, based on regulations and laws. Both doctrine and the Christian way of life are understood within the liturgical context. Within the worshipping community, doctrine *becomes* the action, which constitutes the highest point of the Christian faith.

Thus, the Orthodox approach to both doctrine and the Christian life is fundamentally a liturgical one.[3]

Such an understanding of prayer and worship imposes on us an analogous attitude – and challenge. If prayer follows right faith, it ceases to be a superficial need for a sentimental and shallow communion with God and becomes *true* communion, based on the free acceptance of ecclesiastical doctrine. This means that common prayer is possible for all those who participate in, and are sympathetic to, the same faith. As extreme as this may seem, it has its theological foundation in the premise that dogma and worship are two aspects of one and the same truth. Although these are not two extremities constraining the life of the Church, they are a common basis connecting all human aspects in order to form one body, the Body of Christ.

For the Orthodox it is self-evident that theology, as *God's doxology,* does not have the characteristics of an individual, monistic dialogue between the theologizing person and God; and although personhood maintains its integrity, it is an ecclesial offering. That is to say, the person who theologizes uses his or her own theology to apprehend the mind of the ecclesial body, and then offers it to God in a unique and personal manner. I believe that this ecclesial conscience of theology and prayer is expressed in the liturgy immediately before confessing our common faith in the triune God through the creed, when we urge: "Let us love one another that with one mind we may confess the Father, the Son and the Holy Spirit."[4]

Ecumenical Joint Prayer and Certain Questions about the Orthodox

ECUMENICAL joint prayer has been viewed with scepticism in the past few years by certain Orthodox believers, and even Churches. The reasons for this scepticism are connected with history and, at the same time, have been strengthened by today's ecumenical activity. We need to appreciate that today's reaction has its historical foundation. The Orthodox Churches, presumably not without justification, have related common prayer to proselytism. In particular, over the past three centuries the Orthodox East became an area of activity for Western missionary efforts. Organized Roman Catholic and Protestant missions arrived in Orthodox countries which, for historical reasons, experienced various difficulties, and were offered by the missionaries the prospect of a better way of life. The missions organized schools, founded hospitals and other public welfare institutions. Parallel to various religious gatherings, which were usually limited to common prayer, they operated indeed as "missions": in other words, they practised proselytism by taking advantage of (to some degree) the *naïveté* and indigence of the people.

Thus, to a large portion of the Orthodox, common prayer is associated with a tactic that was not always open and transparent.

On the other hand, in recent years there has been an increasing heaviness of the spiritual climate during ecumenical prayers brought about by certain spurious developments. As stated in the report of sub-committee III of the Special Commission on Orthodox Participation in the World Council of Churches (WCC), which met in Crete in August 2000, "Orthodox participants have found certain elements within the worship activity of the WCC to be incompatible with apostolic tradition. These include (a) the use of inclusive language in referring to God, (b) the leadership of services by ordained women, (c) the introduction of syncretistic elements."

All of this, in the conscience of certain Orthodox, made common prayer difficult. The question often asked is, What meaning does a "fabricated" prayer have if this prayer does not express one united ethos, but is rather a joining together of elements from various ecclesiastical traditions? If prayer is a true doxological expression of ecclesiastical teaching and life, then *which* common faith and common ethos does joint prayer express? Naturally, these questions are not accepted by all. Nonetheless, they are in fact asked and do create a negative climate in the Orthodox world, producing an image of ecumenical work which of course is inconsistent with, and does not correspond to, the visions of the pioneers of ecumenism.

Joint Prayer and Heresy

It is often the case that those who are against common prayer at ecumenical gatherings and theological dialogues emphasize ecclesiastical laws which forbid joint prayer with heretics (for example Apostolic 45, Laodicea 34). Such a correlation is wrong, and we must confirm this with theological reasoning. First of all, the canons which refer to joint prayer with heretics have one specific historical context within which they were published. That is, they were published by the Church to measure the consequences, for the body of the Church, resulting from joint prayers with individuals who disputed *basic dogmas* of the Christian faith, such as the divinity of Christ or God's triune nature.

A mistake made by those who appeal to these canons with regard to common prayer is that they ignore or fail to appreciate the fact that the *Church* gave those canons. Therefore, the canons are not "above" the Church, but the Church is above the canons, which she herself has used, and continues to use, to ease the lives of her faithful. These canons are aimed at specific situations, and cannot be used without condition, or to limit the Church and to subordinate the Church to regulations that she herself has given. It constitutes a basic ecclesiastical principle for Orthodox theology that the Church is the great mystery in which the world is engaged and blessed. The Church, as theanthropic, finds those secure means which look forward to the salvation of humanity. However, in no circumstances can decisions and canons be used as a substitute for the Church, or subordinate it.

Another matter we must face is the topic of heresy and who is called a "heretic". Those who are against joint prayer in ecumenical gatherings and dialogues take for granted that whoever is not in communion with the Orthodox Church is a heretic. Therefore there exists today, as in the past, a number of Orthodox who consider the Roman Catholics and Protestants to be heretics. Based on this drastic simplification, they declare that joint prayer with heretics is forbidden. We must note at this point that ill-advised and impulsive actions of certain persons in the ecumenical movement contributed to this simplification. These were persons who did not hesitate to create "common prayers" in which were found an assortment of cultural and religious elements, and in which the message of the gospel was ultimately vanishing.

It is imperative for us to underline here the fact that there are *no* official synodical pan-Orthodox decisions which characterize Roman Catholics or Protestants as heretics; there are only those statements of individual ecclesiastical writers mentioned today by all those who are against common prayer. In practice there exist among the Orthodox those who are in support of the exact application of the holy canons, and those who follow "an approach of economy" [*oikonomia*]. It must also be added that those in favour of common prayer at ecumenical gatherings and

theological dialogues usually have the consent of the Church
which they represent.

The Church Canons and their Character

IN the life of the Church, already from its earliest years, the
canons have been the origin of "economy" and have been a means
of philanthropy. The canons aim to make the lives of the faithful
easier, to give a measure for Christian behaviour and conduct.
The canons were always the means with which, and the ways by
which, the Church protected the life of its children. Truly, the
canons were for the faithful and not the faithful for the canons.
That is to say, for the canons to have been published and applied
there must have been certain reasons, and appropriate circumstances, which forced the Church in specific situations to carve
out the road which the faithful were obligated to follow. In other
words, without certain preconditions, the canons would not have
been published and there would have been no reason for them to
have been applied. This is also apparent from the fact that when
the reasons which had demanded the publication and application of a particular canon no longer existed, this canon remained
useless, that is, ineffectual – though without being abolished.
Also, in peculiar circumstances the Church has retained the right
to override a canon. A classic example of this occurred during the
German occupation of Greece, when there was massive depri-
vation and hunger, causing many to perish from famine. In this
particular circumstance, the holy synod of the Church of Greece
asked the faithful to eat meat – or anything else that causes one to
break a fast – during the fasting periods.

Thus the canons which forbid joint prayer with heretics,
as well as those that forbid someone to eat with or travel with
heretics, have their historical context and were prescribed by the
specific conjunction of circumstances of that epoch. Although
these canons are not now in effect, they are also not abolished,
and could be applied again, if the peculiar set of circumstances
that originally prescribed their introduction reappeared in the
life of the Church. Nevertheless, it is important for us to clarify

and repeat that the canons do not constrain the Church which created them, nor do they force the Church into a situation from which she cannot escape. Such a notion introduces legalism into the Church, which does not allow space for the life and freedom of grace.

On the basis of this way of thinking, we can say that the Church is able to affirm the disuse of certain canons, in order to highlight her evangelical message. The issue of the *unity* of Christians, which is the context *within* which ecumenical efforts are made, and which is the aim of the theological dialogues, has of course – and should have – priority over any application of edicts. Without wishing to diminish the importance of Church canons in any way, we should note that it is wrong to isolate and absolutize canonical tradition. Today, therefore, as in the past, the Church has an obligation to take a positive stand on existing historical opportunities and, above all, to respond to the calling of Christ, "that they may all be one" (John 17:21).

The fact that the Church has such flexibility in its course of action is evident from the study of church history. It is well-known, and it remains true to this day, that the baptized are members of the Church and have always engaged in joint prayer – and engage in joint prayer nowadays – with those who have not yet been added to the ecclesiastical family. In the Divine Liturgy of Saint John Chrysostom and in the other liturgies, before the eucharistic ceremony there is a common prayer of the catechumens and faithful. The catechumens engage in joint prayer with the faithful, and listen together to the Bible readings. The catechumens are not members of the Church and may originate from heretical backgrounds, or they may even emanate from the pagan world. Nevertheless, the Church does not hesitate to accept them and to offer them the affection of the Church's prayer, since they have expressed their willingness to become her members. It is recognized here that, even given the existence of canons in relation to joint prayer, it all depends on the peculiar set of circumstances. Specifically, it is understood that the Church has the right, and the authority, to judge the circumstances and to decide accord-

ingly. This confirms the view that it is the Church which has the
authority either to impose her canons, or to follow a different
course of action. The same was true in the case of those who repented in the
ancient church. Certain members of the Church, during periods
of persecution, and from fear or cowardice, had renounced the
Christian faith. This was considered a heavy offence and the
Church cut off from her body those who had renounced her.
But later, when certain of them repented of their action and
wanted to return to the body of the faithful, the Church set for
them a period of trials. During this period, those repenting were
accepted into joint prayer but not into eucharistic communion.
Thus the Church did not judge with a legal mentality, but on the
basis of spiritual interest and with that conscience of our God
and Saviour, "who desires all men to be saved and to come to the
knowledge of the truth" (1 Tim. 2:4).

The Nature of Joint Prayer in the Ecumenical Movement

I BELIEVE it is apparent, after all that has been noted, that joint
prayer in the ecumenical movement and the theological dialogues
has both a particular and a specific mission to ease the approach
of Christians from various traditions to one another. This does
not imply that joint prayer is a "means" and tool of compromise
and a diplomatic method of proceeding. The matter is simple: in
our effort to develop and enhance dialogue and understanding of
one another through serious study and an approach to the historical obstacles between us, and also in order for us to observe in
a balanced way the dogmatic differences *within* the ecclesiastical tradition, we need to plead together for divine assistance.
This does not suggest a mentality of compromise, or contempt
for the ecclesiastical canons. It does demonstrate, however, the
freedom of the Church to deal with the issues which occur in its
experience in history with a disposition to love, and with the goal
of the spiritual benefit of the body of the Church. Inasmuch as
the Church has the capability – and also the duty – to survey the
challenges of the times, and deal with them accordingly, it ensures

its own pre-eminence. The Church, as the Body of Christ, is filled with the Holy Trinity, and without altering its dogmatic heritage and its ethos, is of course capable of making decisions in order to deal with new situations and phenomena which have no precedent in Church history. In this perspective, certainly the ecumenical movement and the theological dialogues offer a new reality and opportunity for an Orthodox witness to the truth.

NOTES

* This paper was originally presented to the Special Commission on Orthodox Participation in the World Council of Churches (WCC), meeting in Berekfürdö, Hungary, 15–20 November 2001, and was first published in *The Ecumenical Review* 53 (2002), 33–37.

1. *On Prayer* (PG 19:1180B).

2. G. Every, *The Byzantine Patriarchate* (London, 1974), p. ix; quoted in T. Ware, *The Orthodox Church* (London, 1969), p. 271.

3. See my "Doxology, the Language of Orthodoxy"; originally published in *The Greek Orthodox Theological Review* 38 (1993), 55–56 [reprinted in the present edition].

4. *Liturgy of Saint John Chrysostom.*

Christ and Culture*

THE QUESTION OF THE PERSON OF CHRIST HAS
been a dominant theme running throughout the entire
history of Christianity, both eastern and western. This is
understandable, given that the Person of Christ is the Focus and
ultimate End of the Christian life. The ecclesial life is so inextricably
interwoven with Christ that our vision of his Person contains within
itself our vision of the Church. In the entire New Testamental
and patristic tradition the inseparability of the Person of Christ,
the incarnate Logos, and of the Church is clearly stressed. Saint
Gregory of Nyssa in particular draws special attention to the fact that
"in many instances the Church is called Christ by Saint Paul".[1] Again,
he also states that "he who sees the Church sees Christ before him".[2]
The ecclesial life is nothing less and can be nothing more than a
unique and living communion with Christ.

   We may start our discussion by asking an essential question: What
does the Church offer to the world that was previously unknown?
Put more simply: What is new and unique in Christianity? The
answer is Jesus Christ, the incarnate Word of God. The uniqueness of the Christian Gospel lies in the fact that it introduces
into the world neither a new *theologia speculativa* nor a new *theologia*

practica, but a unique and new reality, the Hypostasis or the fact of Jesus Christ.

Saint Symeon the New Theologian expressed it well when he said: "The beginning is Christ, the midpoint is Christ and the completion is Christ as well; he who is within the first things is in everything: in the midpoint and in the end as in the first things. Christ is all and in all" (Col. 3:11).[3]

For Christians, the Person of Christ is both the great paradox and the great miracle. Christ overcomes death and gives birth to a new reality. Approaching the fact of Christ we cannot ignore the central event of his resurrection. The unchangeable sum of the Christian faith is the belief in the resurrection of Christ. "If Christ be not raised, your faith is vain" (1 Cor. 15:17). The preaching of the Gospel is given forth from the empty grave, and again the Church of Christ is founded on the empty tomb. The reaction of the people, when the Apostle Peter preached the resurrection of Christ in Jerusalem, is striking: " . . .they were pricked in their heart, and said unto Peter and to the rest of the apostles, Men and brethren, what shall we do? Then Peter said unto them, Repent, and be baptized every one of you in the name of Jesus Christ for the remission of sins, and ye shall receive the gift of the Holy Ghost" (Acts 2:37–38).

For the Christian community Christ is not simply a teacher or a lawgiver; he is the eternal Son of God, the *Kyrios* of glory, who through his incarnation allowed himself to become part of human history. The existential involvement of the Son of God in human history implies that the Christian Way is not simply a matter of accepting certain theoretical axioms about God, but primarily it is another mode of existence. The Church is basically communion with him who is the revealer of all truths, creator of a new life, redeemer and saviour. In other words, the incarnate Logos becomes the ontological basis of the new Christian communion. This means that there can be ecclesial communion because there is Christ. This "communion" is understood as an absolutely new situation, created by God's *kenotic* going out of himself, and by the redemptive indwelling of Christ in human reality.

Before getting to grips with the issue "Christ and Culture", I feel that it is necessary to make clear that one cannot present an adequate record concerning the Person of Christ outside the ecclesial experience and reality. We cannot get away from the central fact of the ecclesial dimension. Christology is not the consequence of a particular external and speculative, in the narrow sense, teaching. Nor is it an alternative system of ideas concerning a spiritual leader. One can only have a vital consideration of Jesus Christ, His life, His message, His deeds, when one bases oneself on the *traditio veritatis ecclesiae.*

The ecclesiological approach of Christology protects our understanding from individualistic exercises and from the incli- nation to consider the divine Person of the incarnate *Logos* simply as a phenomenon among others, who introduced new ideas, and new moral and social principles. The ecclesiological dimension protects us also from a monistic understanding of the Person of Christ. "Christomonism" is the consequence of the absence of an orthodox ecclesiology. It has been said in many ways, since earliest Christian tradition, that the Church is a *symbiosis* and a *communion* of believers in the image of the divine communion. She is the reflection of uncreated divine reality in the created human situation. This results in the Church's teaching concerning the Person of Christ being inextricably bound up with her teaching about the One God in Trinity. It is for precisely this reason that in the patristic tradition, especially the Cappadocian, one finds a strong relationship and connection between Christology and Trinitarian theology.

At any rate, the point I am trying to clarify is that Christology cannot be conceived of apart from ecclesiology; and that Christology is always related to Trinitarian theology. These affirmations form a preliminary to what we shall go on to consider. Having made this clear, we shall now proceed to study the question of Christ, or Christianity and Culture.

It is well known that during the first Christian centuries we have a coming together of two worlds, the new of the Gospel and the ancient world of Judaic and Graeco-Roman culture. This meeting of the two different mentalities and traditions was not an easy one. Often the two worlds had come into deep conflict and stood opposed to each another.[4] But nevertheless it is historically wrong to overestimate and absolutize the conflict and consider it as a kind of unbridgeable gulf. Basically the Church did not deny the cultural inheritance. She always was, in principle, open to embrace culture. We should say rather that there is an absolute and negative reaction against Christ from outside the Church world, ancient and modern. Richard Niebuhr puts it well: "Not only Jews but also Greeks and Romans, medievalists and moderns, Westerners and Orientals have rejected Christ because they saw in him a threat to their culture. The story of Graeco-Roman civilization's attack on the gospel forms one of the dramatic chapters in every history of Western culture and of the church, though it is told too often in terms of a political persecution only . . . Ancient spiritualists and modern materialists plus Romans who charge Christianity with atheism, and nineteenth century atheists who condemn its theistic faith, nationalists and humanists, all seem to be offended by the same elements in the gospel and employ arguments in defending their culture against it."[5]

The study of early Christian thought would contribute to the Gospel and culture debate of our time. And even though it is not the scope of this short paper to enter into historical details, I think that a brief reference to the early Christian period would be useful for our discussion. Studying the data from the life of the Early Church one would easily come to the conclusion that although culture has in principle been positively considered, it was never understood as an unconditional good. Civilization meant basically, at the very first Christian epoch, the Hellenic inheritance with all its philosophical trends, social structure and aesthetical charms. One of the first in favour of this Hellenic culture was Justin the Apologist and Martyr who declared that: "The lessons of Plato are not alien from those of Christ, although they are not totally similar. The same is true for the stoics and the poets and the ancient writers. Whatever things have been rightly said by anyone belongs to us Christians".[6]

The same line was, more or less, followed by the theologians of the Alexandrian School. Their attitude was very much in favour of Greek philosophy. Clement understands history as a unique reality, because all truth is one. The Old Testament and Greek philosophy as well were considered as ways leading to Christ. "There is but one way of truth like a river", says Clement, "but many streams fall into it on this side and on that." Clement underlines the paedagogic dimension of philosophy but at the same time recognizes the limited function of it.[7] In Origen's entire theological work and in his relation with the Greek philosophers of his time one sees the presence of the "Christ and culture" issue. Origen recognizes the validity of the Hellenic philosophical tradition, but at the same time he is far more biblical and ecclesiastical. In the overall *schema* of his thought we find three progressive revelations of God: the so-called natural, that of the prophets, and finally the Gospel, in which we see Christ, our teacher and our example.

The Christ and culture question appears also in the efforts of the Greek Fathers, especially those of the Fourth Century, to present the Christian Faith in a language and formulation accessible to the people of God. It is true that the Fathers did not hesitate to use the terminology and categories of Greek thought in order to speak about the Person of Christ and his message. But it is also true that they were very critical of and resisted and denied the pagan Graeco-Roman civilization. They were open to embracing all those things which were considered positive to the *preparatio et interpretatio Evangelica,* but at the same time they stood opposed to the pagan culture. Significant to this attitude is a treatise written by Saint Basil the Great under the title: "To young men, on how they might derive benefit from Hellenic literature."

The Fathers of that period were facing a complex and peculiar situation. A considerable number of intellectuals were worshipping the dead Olympian gods. Numerous pagan temples and schools were maintaining the pagan traditions. Julian the Apostate was not simply an unrealistic dreamer, but an example of cultural resistance. He represented a world that was not yet totally dead. In fact this period was a period of evolution, transformation and revaluation; a period of assimilation. The Christian reception of Hellenic culture should be understood as a "conversion of Hellenism". "The process", writes Fr. Georges Florovsky, "was slow and dramatic, and finally resolved in the birth of a new civilization, which we may describe as Byzantine. One has to realise that there was but one Christian civilization for centuries, the same for the East and the West, and this civilization was born and made in the East. A specific Western civilization came much later. Rome itself was quite Byzantine even in the eighth century. The Byzantine epoch starts if not with Constantine himself, in any case with Theodosius, and reaches its climax under Justinian. His was the time when a Christian culture was conscientiously and deliberately being built and completed as a system. The new culture was a great synthesis in which all the creative traditions and moves of the past were merged and integrated. It was a 'New Hellenism', but a Hellenism drastically christened, as it were, 'churchified'".[8]

The more thoroughly the life and theology of the Early Church is studied the stronger will be the conviction that a new cultural achievement had been realized in the first Christian centuries. We can speak, indeed, of a Christian culture which came out from the Christian-Hellenic debate. It has been rightly said that elements of Hellenic culture were kept and even cherished, but they were drawn into the process of a Christian reinterpretation. It was an acceptance of the postulates of culture and their transvaluation.[9]

To conclude this short historical overview, we could say that the Fathers of the Early Church, moving between the poles of the evangelical truth and civilization, were absolutely convinced that the Christian Gospel was central and dominant in everybody's life. The Gospel, the good news, was Christ himself, who "was made flesh, and dwelt among us" (John 1:14); he came to this world that he might bring human beings to God. We have to estimate within this framework the several modifications of the Christ and culture issue in the early Christian tradition, and bear in mind that loyalty to Jesus Christ was never questioned by faithful Christians. Those, like the Gnostics, who tried to interpret Christ wholly and exclusively in cultural terms, trying to eliminate any tension between him and the several customs and social beliefs, were simply considered, by the main body of the Church, as heretics and alien to the Christian community.[10] There can be no doubt that the Church of the Apostles and of the Fathers, as an historical community, was open to cultural achievement, but at the same time was obedient and dedicated to the truth of Jesus Christ. And this truth, which is Christ himself rather than anything said about Him, could in no way be subject to syncretism.

We can speak of a convergence of the holy and the cultural which has its roots in the creation of human beings and in the re-creation in Christ. It will be useful at this point to undertake a brief theological explanation which will allow us to have a global understanding of the relationship between Christianity and Culture. What we need is a theology of culture which will help us to correct thinking about what culture is and to what extent this culture can operate in the ecclesial life.

Culture is related to the creativity given to human persons by God himself. In the book of Genesis we find that the Lord God gave Adam the possibility: a) to "tend and keep" Paradise, and b) to give names to the animals (Gen. 2:15, 19). Paul Tillich connects the former with technology and the latter with language. In any case, the fact is that the first human person was given a responsible and creative duty. He was given the task to act as a free person and have a responsible status with regard to the created world.

Language, as a communicative power, and the ability of keeping alive and taking care of the created world – as bestowed on the human person by God – are proofs that for human beings was reserved a divine, so to speak, function and responsibility. Human persons were created by God according to his image and his likeness, in order to realize in the world a creative *diakonia;* a unique service for the preservation and integrity of creation. The human being was called by God to act in the created world as its king, priest and prophet. In this perspective the function of culture has a spiritual and charismatic dimension. This was the primordial vocation and mission of human beings. The essential unity of the gift given by God to humans and their free acceptance of the responsibility to cultivate "the garden" is of substantial importance for the understanding of the meaning of culture. The point is that, concerning the question of culture, one must not overestimate the human element and achievement, but at the same time one should not underestimate and minimize the creative vocation and power bestowed on human beings by God himself.

The substance and destiny of culture is not irrelevant to the original and ultimate vocation of human beings. This means that the content and preordination of culture is very much related to the fact that God "made human nature the participant of every good".[11] Human beings, in their original state, participating in God's perfections, had a dynamic vocation both for a progressive participation of God and dedication and responsibility for a creativity in and consecrating of the world. It seems to me that on this ground lies the justification of culture. Culture is not justified unconditionally; it is not justified on exclusively anthropocentric ground, on a purely theoretical level, *in abstracto,* but precisely because humans received the divine gift of creativity. In other words, culture, in its pure and undefiled form, is related to human authenticity.

By the free acceptance of sin human persons were reduced *qua* persons, and lost their equilibrium. In other words, by sin the very structure of the human being was affected. In Patristic anthropology sin is understood as a catastrophe caused by the free will of intelligent beings. Even the natural world suffers its effect.[12] Thus, the capacity given by God for creativity was obscured and lost its original vitality, validity and dimension. One discussing the question of culture should not ignore this tragedy of the human race. The point is that through sin the human person was divided in its own being, and thus became an alien and a stranger of the original and authentic state of *koinonia.* Consequently, the capacity for creativity was limited and characterized by egocentrism.

It is only through the *kenosis* (the self-emptying) of the Person of the World of God that a re-creation and restructuring of humanity is realized. If by sin an existential change is effected in the very structure of man's existence, the restoration or even

better, the reintegration of the human person results from the
Person of the Incarnate *Logos*. It is a fundamental point of Patristic
anthropology that the eternal Word of God dwelt among us freely
in order to realize in his theandric Person the restoration of the
human person. By taking one concrete and individual human
nature, he healed our humanity. He who is consubstantial with
the Father in his divinity, in becoming consubstantial with us
through his humanity, re-created the human race. There is thus an
anthropological corollary: The true stature of the human person
is exhibited in and through Christ.

On this basis one can establish certain points concerning the
question of Christ and culture:

1) The positive concern for culture is not irrelevant to the
creation of human beings by God himself, who impresses upon them
his own divine image. Equally, this is not irrelevant to their re-
creation by Christ, the incarnate Word, who repaints and restores
the divine image, obscured through sin. From this perspective it
is evident that to the human person, both in creation and in re-
creation in Christ, was given immense potentialities for creating a
personal history of holiness; and at the same time, man is called by
the Maker to meet the needs of his age, and by using the divine gift
of creativity, to build a culture worthy of the original and ultimate
vocation of the human person. Taking historical experience and
the current situation into account, this may be considered impossible, an illusion or a dream. But nevertheless, the vocation of the
human being is to progress, with the help of God, and proceed
from the present state to a state which may be termed transformed
human life. H. R. Niebuhr puts it well: "Human culture can be a
transformed human life in and to the glory of God. For man it is
impossible, but all things are possible for God, who has created
man, body and soul for himself, and sent his Son into the world
that the world through him might be saved".[13]

In the Christian community, even from the days of the Early
Church, theology has had manifold and intimate relations with
culture. This is understandable, given that the Christian *kerygma*
does not do its work in a vacuum. The Gospel has to enter into the

human situation. Theology has the task and duty of penetrating the depths of human history, that means of entering into dialogue with human thought. This does not at all signify a relativism of the Gospel, or an adaptation of the Gospel to every current cultural achievement. It simply means that human thought and, more generally, human culture can be in a certain sense and under certain conditions a *praeparatio evangelica*.

2) As we have already pointed out, over the long course of Christian history the Church's attitude towards culture was not monochrome. Parallel to the positive concern for culture, which is based on the fact that God created human beings in his own image and re-created humanity through the self-emptying of his Son, one finds also a rejection of culture. In radical fashion Tertullian stated in a much quoted text: "What indeed has Athens to do with Jerusalem? What concord is there between the Academy and the Church? ... Our instruction comes from the Porch of Solomon, who had himself taught that the Lord should be sought in simplicity of heart ... We want no curious disputation after possessing Christ Jesus, no inquisition after enjoying the Gospel. With our faith we desire no further belief. For this is our palmary faith, that there is nothing which we ought to believe besides."[14] The same rejection of culture can be found in several Christian circles, even today. To give just one example, the Mennonites represent, from the time of the Reformation until the present day, a purely anti-cultural attitude. They not only exclude from their social system and way of life any participation in politics and all wider social activities, but also follow regulations and principles for education, economy and social life, which are characteristically distinctive of their own mentality and their own understanding of the Gospel.[15] One can find similar examples, less striking perhaps, among the Old Believers in Russia or the Old Calendarists in Greece. In these circles, Christian life is often understood as a life apart from civilization.

This negative, so to speak, attitude towards culture is based on the argument that civilization is not the final goal of human destiny. Culture is composed of various values which were produced during the course of human history. However, from a

Christian point of view, cultural achievements are not the ultimate
values of life; they are often not even necessary presuppositions for
salvation. Fr. Georges Florovsky remarks that "a primitive can be
saved no less than a civilized" person.[16] One can even argue that
it can be perhaps easier for a "primitive" to be saved, given that
he is free from the yoke of civilization, and consequently has
the potential for a clear and direct vision of the Christian truth.
Cultural "accumulations" are often obstacles, which do not allow
the human person to reach the "foolishness" of the Gospel. It is
beyond doubt that "the wisdom of this world is foolishness with
God. For it is written, He taketh the wise in their own craftiness.
And again, The Lord knoweth the thoughts of the wise, that they
are vain" (1 Cor. 3:19–20).[17]

3) From the above-mentioned attitudes or polarities, on the
question of civilization, one sees that culture is neither unconditionally good nor evil *per se*. Culture can be good, a real divine gift,
but it can also be evil, a real demonic power or yoke. It can be a
way leading towards the understanding of the Christian Gospel,
but it can equally be a serious obstacle for reaching the Christian
message. Culture can really facilitate human life and assist human
persons, helping them with their spiritual development, but it
can also alienate them from the genuine human life, not allowing
human persons to realize that their vocation lies in an infinite
progress of their own knowledge and union with God. Culture can
assist human persons in developing their own personal talents,
or it can be a heavy burden, inimical to and restraining human
creativity. In our highly civilized world the spiritual elements are
often inexistent and the human person is hemmed in by the fruits
of his own creation. It has been rightly said that in our times
human beings suffer from the tyranny of cultural routine and from
the bondage of civilization. Often, no room is left for a creative
and authentic human life. It is strange but it is true: culture more
often than not leads towards an uncivilized way of life.

We live in a period of history where human achievements are
absolutized and even deified. It is a period of neo-idolatry, where
a less cultured person is, in many circumstances, considered as a

lesser human being. I believe that this is a problem not only for our secular societies, but also for our secularized churches. Many of the problems our churches are facing today are very much connected with a mentality that places culture at the top of their interests. Christians often forget that culture can only be a means towards Christian understanding, but in no way can it be a substitute of the Christian message. It is our Christian duty to face responsibly the question of culture, and to be aware of its limits. It is our urgent obligation to admit that an overestimation of cultural achievements makes the human person a prisoner of his own attainments. By making culture the centre of human activity and the goal and ground of human existence, we, in fact, make the human person estranged from himself. In this case, the human being is cut off from the main body of his existence; he is separated from God, from his fellow human being, and from nature as well.

In saying all this, I do not intend to anathematize culture as such, neither do I intend to bring back so-called "cultural pessimism". Rather, what I want to say is that we must, as Christians, see the reality of culture in the light of the Christian Gospel. This means that our attitude towards culture should be an ecclesiocentric one. Indeed, within the ecclesial community, Christians can exercise their calling to seek the true value and the boundaries of civilization.

The Church, as the body which is maintained in its integrity by the continuing presence of Christ, has the duty and the responsibility to discern what is faithful to the truth of the Gospel and what is not, what edifies the body and what introduces discord to it. It is only within the ecclesial reality that one can mature and have a right understanding of what is relevant to the Christian message and what is irrelevant, or even opposed to it. "For every one that useth milk is unskilful in the word of righteousness: for he is a babe. But strong meat belongeth to them that are of full age, even those who by reason of use have their senses exercised to discern both good and evil" (Heb. 5:13–14). The Church, perhaps more so today than in any other period of history, should remain faithful to her double vocation: firstly, through her spiritual ability to distinguish and see the differences between good and evil, and secondly, to translate responsibly the fundamental Christian principles in order to meet the challenges of our constantly developing historical context. The Church has exercised this double mission throughout the entire course of history, and has, today as always, the obligation to be faithful to her vocation.

It is evident that we live in a cultural pluralism and we need charismatic, that is to say, ecclesial criteria for the "discerning of spirits" (1 Cor. 12:10). Otherwise, our churches will follow the streams of the world, and adapt their preaching to the desires and customs of the world. If the Church unwisely or carelessly accepts what the contemporary cultural and social currents offer, it is obvious that divisions will arise.

It is true that in our time, as perhaps in every age in history, there is in many cases a radical tension and contrast between the Christian ethos and certain forms of culture. Mechanized culture, the culture that serves totalitarian systems or economic interests, the culture which destroys both the balance and the integrity of the human person or the integrity of the environment, together with certain ideas and actions which, in the name of democracy, of equality and of human rights overthrow the harmony of the human relationship; all of these often have a direct or indirect influence upon the life of our churches. It is important for the being and welfare of the churches to always bear in mind that although they are *in the world* they are not *of the world* (*cf.* John 17:11–14). The constant prayer of Christ for His Church is summarized in His Word addressed to His Father, and preserved by John: "I pray not that thou shouldest take them out of the world, but that thou shouldest keep them from the evil one" (John 17:15).

4) In a period of history, where the human person is more or less enclosed within the narrow limits of exclusively worldly concerns, the Church, remaining faithful to her inheritance, has the calling to preach the Gospel responsibly, that is, to present in this world of ours and in this time of ours the Person of Christ. She cannot give up on the fundamental and ultimate goal of her existence in order to satisfy temporary or worldly concerns. Her

attitude towards culture should be, as always, dialectical: a dialectic of approach and distance, of solidarity and judgment, of close relationship and at the same time of serious criticism. We cannot abandon the ecclesial basis. As it is impossible to reach an orthodox Christology outside the ecclesial life and tradition, likewise it is not possible to have a right judgment concerning human and cultural achievements outside the experience and the doctrine (the *praxis* and *theoria*) of the Church. It is only within the Church that we understand Christ, not simply as a lawgiver or as a religious leader or even as an historic superhuman personality, but as the incarnate eternal Logos of God, who became flesh in order to transform the world and culture.

The promise and profession of the Church *vis-à-vis* culture, and generally *vis-à-vis* the entire human drama, is I think assumed by and summarized in the biblical story of the transfiguration. The constant effort of the ecclesial *diakonia* is to make transfiguration accessible to every current human situation.

When we stress here the event of the transfiguration, in fact we stress the very Person of Jesus Christ. The ecclesial experience is nothing other than a living communion in and through Christ. In this new and unique reality all human actions are transfigured, so that they are acts of love towards God and love towards the image of God, the human being; they are acts which glorify the Father, the Son and the Holy Spirit, and consequently they glorify, respect and honour the human person.

NOTES

* Paper first published in *Evangelisches Missionswerk Informationen* 113 (1996), 28–34.

1. *Life of Moses,* ed. H. Musurillo, p. 95:12–13. PG 44:385A.

2. *On the Song of Songs,* ed. H. Langerbeck, p. 383:3–5. PG 44:1048C.

3. *Practical and Theological Chapters* III, 1.

4. G. Florovsky, "Christianity and Civilization", *Christianity and Culture* (Belmont MA, 1974), p. 121.

5. H. R. Niebuhr, *Christ and Culture* (New York, 1951), pp. 4–5.

6. *Second Apology* 13, 2–4.

7. *Stromateis* 1, 5.

8. Florovsky, *op. cit.*, p. 122.

9. *Ibid.*, p. 123.

10. See Niebuhr, *op. cit.*, p. 85.

11. Gregory of Nyssa, *On the Making of Man* 16. PG 44:184B.

12. C. Scouteris, "The People of God. Its Unity and Its Glory: A Discussion of John 17:17–24 in the Light of Patristic Thought", *The Greek Orthodox Theological Review* 30 (1985), 409 [reprinted in the present edition].

13. Niebuhr, *op. cit.*, p. 196.

14. *The Prescription of Heretics* 1.

15. Niebuhr, *op. cit.*, p. 56.

16. *Op. cit.*, p. 14.

17. See Job 5:13, and Ps. 94:11.